RECIPES

Desserts

ISBN: 978-0-8487-5225-5

ISSN 2471-643X

Library of Congress Control Number:
2017936066

Printed in the United States of America
10 9 8 7 6 5 4 3 2 1
First Edition 2017

FOOD & WINE
DESSERTS

EXECUTIVE EDITOR **Kate Heddings**
EDITOR **Susan Choung**
DESIGNER **Alisha Petro**
COPY EDITOR **Lisa Leventer**
PRODUCTION DIRECTOR **Joseph Colucci**
PRODUCTION MANAGERS **Stephanie Thompson,
John Markic**
EDITORIAL ASSISTANT **Dinavie Salazar**

FRONT COVER
S'mores Bars (recipe, p. 184)
PHOTOGRAPHER **Con Poulos**
FOOD STYLIST **Kay Chun**
STYLE EDITOR **Suzie Myers**

BACK COVER
Ice Cream Birthday Cake (recipe, p. 232)
PHOTOGRAPHER **David Malosh**
FOOD STYLIST **Hadas Smirnoff**
For additional photo contributors, see p. 270.

FOOD & WINE

EDITOR IN CHIEF **Nilou Motamed**
EXECUTIVE EDITOR **Dana Bowen**
ART DIRECTOR **James Maikowski**
PHOTO EDITOR **Sara Parks**
PHOTO ASSISTANT **Rebecca Delman**

FOOD&WINE

Desserts

BY THE EDITORS OF
FOOD & WINE

CONTENTS

Mexican Chocolate Chip–Pumpkin
Seed Cake, p. 40

Creamy Mocha Ice Pops, p. 221

FOREWORD

Trust us, you want this book. Just look at the cover! That's a giant s'mores bar, layered with a crazy-crunchy graham cracker crust, fudgy chocolate filling and a dreamy mile-high meringue. It's an OMG dessert—the kind that wows guests and wins you favorite-host status. Like all the recipes on these pages, it represents our tried-and-true keepers from years of tasting and perfecting in the F&W Test Kitchen. Want the best-of-the-best tarte tatin? Hands down, it's chef Jonathan Waxman's version made with sweet Golden Delicious apples, which hold their shape in the pan (p. 88). Or the holy grail of brownies? Try the salted fudge ones that we bake for every staff gathering, where we fight over the crisp-chewy corners (p. 176).

Several editors happily volunteered to share their go-tos, so you'll find something to satisfy every type of craving. For executive wine editor Ray Isle, who has a mega sweet tooth, his favorites include the super-decadent pecan pie that took home first place in a Texas state fair (p. 130) and the richer-than-Oprah Krispy Kreme bread pudding dolloped with espresso whipped cream (p. 77). Books editor Susan Choung, on the other hand, prefers a savory edge to her desserts. She loves the honey-tahini cookies that she calls "the thinking person's answer to peanut butter cookies" (p. 160) and the hit of tangy sorrel in a lemon sherbet that's the ultimate summer refresher (p. 237). Ever want just one perfect chocolate chip cookie without baking an entire batch? We've got that, too—a pick from associate food editor Julia Heffelfinger (p. 146).

All these and more await you. All told: a pretty sweet deal. Enjoy!

Nilou Motamed
Editor in Chief
FOOD & WINE

Kate Heddings
Executive Editor
FOOD & WINE Cookbooks

Petits Pots à l'Absinthe,
p. 192

THE EATERS

Justin Chapple
Test Kitchen Deputy Editor

As the star of F&W's Mad Genius Tips video series, Justin spends much of his time developing wonderfully oddball cooking hacks in addition to testing and creating hundreds of recipes a year for the magazine.

Favorite Childhood Memories: Being able to buy four avocados for a dollar in his hometown of Stockton and munching on Northern California's best-kept secret—Dutch crunch bread!

Julia Heffelfinger
Associate Food Editor

A proud Minnesotan, Julia always keeps her fridge stocked with M&M's and a half-gallon of milk. She remembers most of the important moments in her life by the food served at the time, and still holds a grudge against her sister for eating the center of her cinnamon roll in 1998. (I'll NEVER forget, Laura.)

Worth Fighting For: She has been known to get into physical altercations over guacamole.

Nilou Motamed
Editor in Chief

Born in Iran and raised in Paris and New York City, Nilou has an equal-opportunity sweet tooth. She'll never turn down Persian rosewater ice cream, delicate French macarons or old-fashioned cider doughnuts warm from the fryer.

Indulgent Breakfast: Her husband Peter's buttermilk pancakes, from his mother's recipe, topped with wild Maine blueberries, cultured butter and plenty of maple syrup.

Susan Choung
Books Editor

Growing up in Brooklyn, New York, Susan helped out at her parents' Italian and Jewish delis. She still has strong opinions about sandwiches.

Regrettable Baking Blunders: Forgetting to whisk the dry ingredients her first time making scones, so just one of them got all the salt. Adding ketchup potato chips to chocolate chip cookie dough; the combo did not go over well.

Ray Isle
Executive Wine Editor

Ray spends an inordinate amount of time cooking, to ensure that he has enough interesting food to pair with all the wine he "has to" taste. It's very important, he likes to point out, to try at least 20 different Syrahs with a leg of lamb you just roasted.

Ultimate Escape: Going to Northeast Harbor, Maine, and kayaking all afternoon out on Somes Sound.

Sara Parks
Photo Editor

Sara grew up in rural western Massachusetts, making pies with her mother. She now bakes on her own in Brooklyn, trying to achieve the flaky layers in her mom's pie crust.

Recent Baking Feats: A bûche de Noël that was a two-day effort, a batch of cherry hand pies involving the fussiest dough and a boozy chocolate cake for New Year's Eve.

Kate Heddings
Executive Food Editor

Kate's love affair with Hostess cupcakes and Suzy Q's as a kid morphed into a passion in adulthood for all things sweet (except fudge). With two kids at home, she definitely favors speedy recipes and has developed a newfound obsession with her rice cooker.

A Perfect Food Day: Kimchi, blue crab, raw green beans and (of course) lots of different desserts to sample.

James Maikowski
Art Director

James, an only child who grew up in the Connecticut River Valley, majored in art at the University of Connecticut. His minor: standing in line at the Dairy Bar (the on-campus scoop shop).

Proudest Food Moment: Mastering his grandmother's recipe for *potica,* a takes-all-day-so-don't-make-any-plans Slovenian yeast bread filled with sweetened nuts.

Christine Quinlan
Deputy Editor

A relentless dessert seeker, Christine has been known to choose vacation spots based on the density of bakeries. As a kid, she'd get in trouble for climbing on counters to sneak cookies.

Sweet Rewards: Her first job was a paper route near Boston, which yielded plenty of tips on collection day to splurge on sticky buns and cupcakes at the corner store.

Cakes & Pastries

DOUBLE-CHOCOLATE LAYER CAKE

MAKES One 8-inch layer cake

TIME Active 40 min; Total 1 hr 30 min plus chilling

CAKE

Unsalted butter, for greasing

1¾ cups all-purpose flour, plus more for dusting

2 cups granulated sugar

¾ cup unsweetened cocoa powder

2 tsp. baking soda

1 tsp. baking powder

1 tsp. kosher salt

1 cup buttermilk

½ cup vegetable oil

2 large eggs

1 tsp. pure vanilla extract

1 cup freshly brewed hot coffee

FROSTING

6 oz. semisweet chocolate, coarsely chopped

2 sticks unsalted butter, at room temperature

1 large egg yolk

1 tsp. pure vanilla extract

1 cup plus 1 Tbsp. confectioners' sugar, sifted

1 Tbsp. instant coffee granules

Who doesn't love cake? Especially this moist, chocolaty one from Food Network star Ina Garten. When she demoed the recipe on her show, the live audience was so happy with it that she describes them as "face down on the cake." The secret: Coffee in the batter as well as the frosting keeps the sweetness in check.

1 MAKE THE CAKE Preheat the oven to 350°. Butter two 8-inch round cake pans and line the bottoms with parchment; butter the paper. Dust the pans with flour, tapping out any excess.

2 In the bowl of a stand mixer fitted with the paddle, mix the 1¾ cups of flour with the granulated sugar, cocoa powder, baking soda, baking powder and salt at low speed. In a medium bowl, whisk the buttermilk with the oil, eggs and vanilla. Slowly beat the buttermilk mixture into the dry ingredients until just incorporated, then slowly beat in the hot coffee until fully incorporated.

3 Pour the batter into the prepared pans and bake for 35 minutes, until a toothpick inserted in the center of each cake comes out clean. Let the cakes cool in the pans for 30 minutes, then invert them onto a rack to cool. Peel off the parchment.

4 MAKE THE FROSTING In a microwave-safe bowl, heat the chocolate at high power for 30 seconds at a time, stirring in between, until most of the chocolate is melted. Stir until completely melted, then set aside to cool.

5 In the cleaned bowl of the stand mixer fitted with the paddle, beat the 2 sticks of butter at medium speed until pale and fluffy. Add the egg yolk and vanilla and beat for 1 minute, scraping down the bowl. At low speed, slowly beat in the confectioners' sugar, about 1 minute. In a small bowl, dissolve the instant coffee in 2 teaspoons of hot water. Slowly beat the coffee and the cooled chocolate into the butter mixture until just combined.

6 Set a cake layer on a plate with the flat side facing up. Evenly spread one-third of the frosting over the cake to the edge. Top with the second cake layer, rounded side up. Spread the remaining frosting over the top and sides of the cake. Refrigerate for at least 1 hour before slicing.

MAKE AHEAD

The frosted cake can be refrigerated for up to 2 days. Let stand for 1 hour before serving.

> "I'm always on the lookout for good desserts to make for my nephew, who has celiac disease, and this one's a keeper. It's supremely moist, with a texture almost like pound cake. You can't tell it's gluten-free, which is the highest compliment you can give a GF cake."
>
> —SUSAN CHOUNG, BOOKS EDITOR

CHOCOLATE, CINNAMON AND ALMOND LOAF CAKE

SERVES 8 to 10

TIME Active 20 min;
Total 2 hr

Nonstick baking spray

2½ cups superfine almond meal

½ cup unsweetened Dutch-process cocoa powder, sifted

2 tsp. baking powder

½ tsp. kosher salt

2½ tsp. cinnamon

6 large eggs, separated

1 cup coconut palm sugar

½ stick unsalted butter, melted and cooled slightly

½ cup cooled brewed coffee

2 tsp. pure vanilla extract

1 cup heavy cream

Julia Turshen, author of *Small Victories*, gives chocolate cake a healthy makeover by replacing white flour with almond meal and swapping out white sugar for coconut sugar. When she's making the cake for her diabetic wife, Grace, she uses only ¼ cup of sweetener, but for a more traditionally sweet cake, 1 cup is just right.

1 Preheat the oven to 350°. Grease a 9-by-5-inch loaf pan with nonstick spray and line it with parchment paper, allowing 2 inches of overhang on the short sides.

2 In a medium bowl, whisk the almond meal, cocoa powder, baking powder, salt and 1½ teaspoons of the cinnamon. In a large bowl, whisk the egg yolks with the coconut sugar, melted butter, coffee and vanilla. Stir the dry ingredients into the wet ingredients until the batter is smooth.

3 In a stand mixer fitted with the whisk, beat the egg whites at medium-high speed until stiff peaks form, 1 to 2 minutes. Fold one-third of the beaten egg whites into the batter to lighten it, then fold in the remaining egg whites until no streaks remain.

4 Scrape the batter into the prepared pan and bake for 45 to 50 minutes, until a toothpick inserted in the center comes out with a few crumbs attached. Transfer to a rack to cool for 20 minutes, then unmold, remove the parchment paper and let cool completely.

5 Meanwhile, in a medium bowl, beat the heavy cream with the remaining 1 teaspoon of cinnamon until soft peaks form. Cut the cake into slices and serve with a dollop of the cinnamon cream.

MAKE AHEAD

The cake can be stored in an airtight container overnight.

TRIPLE-LAYER CHOCOLATE MACAROON CAKE

SERVES 8

TIME Active 35 min;
Total 3 hr 45 min

Nonstick cooking spray

1⅔ cups heavy cream

10½ oz. bittersweet chocolate, chopped

3½ oz. milk chocolate, chopped

4 large eggs

1½ cups sugar

4⅔ cups dried unsweetened finely grated coconut (10 oz.)

Chocolate curls, for garnish

The beauty of this recipe from renowned French pastry chef François Payard lies in its elegant simplicity: Just six ingredients yield a chewy coconut cake layered with silky, rich chocolate ganache.

1 Preheat the oven to 350°. Coat an 11-by-17-inch jelly-roll pan with nonstick spray and line the bottom with parchment paper; spray the paper.

2 In a small saucepan, bring the cream to a boil. Remove from the heat, add the chocolates and let stand for 5 minutes, then whisk until smooth. Pour 1 cup of the chocolate ganache into a measuring cup and set aside at room temperature; scrape the rest into a bowl. Cover the bowl with plastic wrap and refrigerate the ganache until firm, at least 3 hours.

3 In a medium saucepan, bring 1 inch of water to a bare simmer. Using a hand mixer, beat the eggs and sugar in a large bowl at medium speed until blended. Set the bowl over the simmering water and whisk until the eggs are warm to the touch. Remove from the heat and beat at high speed until tripled in volume, about 5 minutes. Fold in 3⅔ cups of the coconut. Spread the batter evenly in the prepared pan and bake for about 25 minutes, until golden and firm. Let the cake cool for 15 minutes.

4 Run a knife around the edge of the cake; invert it onto a baking sheet and peel off the parchment. Slide the cake onto a work surface. Using a serrated knife, trim the edges and cut the cake into 3 rectangles of equal size. Stack the layers and trim off any uneven sides with the knife.

5 Set a cake layer smooth side up on a wire rack and spread with half of the chilled ganache. Cover with a second layer and the remaining chilled ganache. Top with the third cake layer, smooth side up; press down gently. Pour half of the reserved ganache on top and spread it evenly, letting it drip slightly down the sides. Pour on the remaining ganache and smooth the top and sides. Transfer the cake to a cake plate. Refrigerate for 15 minutes, then press the remaining coconut onto the sides of the cake. Garnish with chocolate curls and serve, or, for best results, refrigerate the cake overnight.

MAKE AHEAD

The cake can be refrigerated for up to 4 days.

VANILLA BEAN CAKE WITH SALTED CARAMEL SAUCE

MAKES   One 9-inch cake

TIME   Active 30 min;
         Total 2 hr

CAKE

- 2 sticks unsalted butter, softened, plus more for greasing
- 2½ cups all-purpose flour, plus more for dusting
- 1 tsp. baking powder
- 1 tsp. salt
- 1 cup granulated sugar
- ½ cup brown sugar
- 4 large eggs
- ¼ cup crème fraîche or sour cream
- 3 Tbsp. vanilla paste (see Note) or 1 vanilla bean, split and seeds scraped

CARAMEL SAUCE

- ¾ cup heavy cream
- ¾ cup light corn syrup
- 1¼ cups granulated sugar
- 4 Tbsp. unsalted butter
- ¼ tsp. sea salt

NOTE

Vanilla paste is available at specialty food shops.

Valerie Gordon of Valerie Confections in L.A. glazes her fabulous vanilla cake with a buttery caramel sauce that drips down the sides. "I tried making this as an upside-down cake, which was a disaster, but then I realized I could just pour the caramel on top," she says.

1 MAKE THE CAKE Preheat the oven to 350° and butter and flour a 9-inch round cake pan. In a medium bowl, whisk the 2½ cups of flour with the baking powder and salt. In a large bowl, using a hand mixer, beat the 2 sticks of butter at medium speed until creamy. Add both sugars and beat until fluffy. Add the eggs 1 at a time, beating well between additions, then add the crème fraîche and vanilla. At medium-low speed, beat in the dry ingredients until smooth and evenly combined.

2 Scrape the batter into the prepared pan and smooth the surface. Bake in the center of the oven for about 1 hour, until the cake is golden and springy and a toothpick inserted in the center comes out with a few moist crumbs attached. Let the cake cool in the pan for 20 minutes. Turn the cake out onto a plate, then invert onto a rack and let cool.

3 MEANWHILE, MAKE THE SAUCE In a microwave-safe cup, combine the cream and corn syrup. In a medium, wide saucepan, spread the sugar in an even layer. Cook over moderate heat, without stirring, until it begins to caramelize. Swirl the pan and stir to incorporate the caramelized sugar. At this point, microwave the cream mixture at high power for 2 minutes. Continue cooking the sugar until a medium-amber caramel forms, about 4 minutes. Remove the pan from the heat and carefully add the hot cream, stirring with a long-handled spoon. Return the caramel to low heat and add the butter and salt, stirring until any hardened caramel is melted. Transfer the caramel to a heatproof glass jar and let cool.

4 Poke the top of the cake all over with a skewer and pour 1 cup of the caramel sauce over the cake, allowing it to seep in and drip down the sides. Reserve the rest for another use. Cut the cake into wedges and serve.

PREP AHEAD

The unglazed cake can be stored in an airtight container at room temperature for up to 3 days. The sauce can be refrigerated for up to 1 month. Rewarm before serving.

FOUR-LAYER COCONUT CAKE

MAKES One 8-inch layer cake

TIME Active 1 hr;
Total 2 hr plus cooling

CAKE

- 1½ sticks unsalted butter, at room temperature, plus more for greasing
- 24 oz. unsweetened flaked coconut
- 2¼ cups cake flour
- 2 tsp. baking powder
- ½ tsp. baking soda
- ¼ cup virgin coconut oil
- 1½ cups sugar
- ½ tsp. kosher salt
- ¼ tsp. ground cardamom
- 3 large eggs
- 1¼ cups buttermilk

FROSTING

- 2 cups sugar
- 3 Tbsp. honey
- 6 large egg whites
- ¼ tsp. plus ⅛ tsp. kosher salt
- ¼ tsp. plus ⅛ tsp. cream of tartar
- One 12-oz. jar orange marmalade

Michelle Polzine makes Eastern European–inspired desserts at her 20th Century Cafe in San Francisco's Hayes Valley, but for this showstopper she looks to the American South. She amps up the batter with coconut oil and toasted ground coconut, then decorates the cake with bittersweet marmalade, mounds of honey-sweetened frosting and more toasted coconut.

1 MAKE THE CAKE Preheat the oven to 350°. Grease two 8-inch round cake pans and line the bottoms with parchment paper.

2 Place 4 cups of the coconut in a blender; pulse until finely ground. Spread the ground coconut on a baking sheet. On another baking sheet, spread the remaining coconut. Toast both sheets for 7 to 8 minutes, stirring occasionally, until lightly golden; let cool.

3 Into a large bowl, sift the cake flour, baking powder and baking soda. In another large bowl, using a hand mixer, cream the 1½ sticks of butter with the coconut oil, sugar, salt and cardamom at medium-high speed until light, about 3 minutes. Beat in the toasted ground coconut. Beat in the eggs 1 at a time until incorporated. At low speed, beat in the dry ingredients and buttermilk in 3 alternating batches, starting and ending with the flour.

4 Divide the batter between the pans and bake for 50 to 60 minutes, until the cakes are deep golden and springy. Transfer the cakes to a rack and let cool. Turn the cakes out and peel off the parchment. Cut each cake in half horizontally to create 4 layers.

5 MAKE THE FROSTING In a large saucepan, boil the sugar, honey and ¾ cup of water over moderately high heat until the syrup registers 240° on a candy thermometer. Meanwhile, in the bowl of a stand mixer fitted with the whisk, beat the egg whites at medium speed until foamy; beat in the salt and cream of tartar until soft peaks form. With the mixer on, drizzle the hot syrup down the side of the bowl. Once all of the syrup has been added, beat the frosting at high speed until shiny and thick, about 11 minutes. Let cool.

6 Set a cake layer cut side up on a plate. Spread one-third of the marmalade over the top, then spread with ½ cup of the frosting; repeat with 2 more cake layers. Top with the last layer. Coat the cake with the remaining frosting. Cover with the toasted coconut and serve.

MAKE AHEAD

The cake can be refrigerated for up to 2 days.

MAPLE-BOURBON BANANA PUDDING CAKE

SERVES **6**

TIME **Active 15 min; Total 1 hr**

- 6 **Tbsp. unsalted butter**
- ½ **cup superfine sugar**
- 1 **overripe banana, mashed**
- 1 **large egg**
- 1 **cup whole milk, at room temperature**
- 1 **cup all-purpose flour**
- 1 **Tbsp. baking powder**
  Pinch of salt
- ¾ **cup pure maple syrup**
- ½ **cup light brown sugar**
- 2 **Tbsp. bourbon**
- ¼ **cup finely chopped pecans**
  Vanilla ice cream, for serving

You'll never have to worry about a dry cake with this recipe—it's almost like a bread pudding. Cookbook author Grace Parisi drizzles bourbon-spiked maple syrup over the batter so that a sweet, rich sauce forms in the bottom of the dish as the cake bakes. It's irresistible served warm with vanilla ice cream.

1 Preheat the oven to 375°. In a deep 2-quart baking or soufflé dish, melt the butter in the microwave. Whisk in the superfine sugar and banana, mashing until thoroughly combined. Whisk in the egg and milk.

2 In a bowl, whisk the flour, baking powder and salt; whisk into the baking dish until combined (the batter will be pretty loose).

3 In a microwave-safe cup, heat the maple syrup, brown sugar and ½ cup of hot water at high power until hot, about 1 minute. Add the bourbon. Drizzle the syrup mixture over the batter; it will seep to the bottom. Do not stir. Scatter the pecans on top.

4 Set the dish on a rimmed baking sheet and bake for 40 minutes, until the cake is golden. Let cool for 5 minutes, then scoop into bowls and serve with ice cream.

CLASSIC CARROT CAKE WITH FLUFFY CREAM CHEESE FROSTING

SERVES **8 to 10**

TIME **Active 40 min;
Total 3 hr 30 min**

CAKE

   Unsalted butter, for greasing

2 **cups all-purpose flour, plus
more for dusting**

1 **cup pecans (4 oz.)**

2 **tsp. baking powder**

2 **tsp. baking soda**

1 **tsp. cinnamon**

1 **tsp. salt**

1 **cup vegetable oil**

½ **cup buttermilk**

1½ **tsp. pure vanilla extract**

4 **large eggs**

2 **cups granulated sugar**

1 **lb. carrots, peeled and coarsely
shredded**

FROSTING

2 **sticks unsalted butter, softened**

16 **oz. cream cheese, softened**

1 **Tbsp. pure vanilla extract**

2 **cups confectioners' sugar**

📷 PAGE 13

Carrot cake, that 1970s favorite, has found a new generation of devotees. At Bribery Bakery in Austin, Jodi Elliott prepares a stellar version: layers of super-moist, not-too-sweet cake iced with the perfect cream cheese frosting. You're gonna love it.

1 MAKE THE CAKE Preheat the oven to 325°. Butter two 9-inch round cake pans and line the bottoms with parchment. Butter the paper and flour the pans.

2 Spread the pecans on a baking sheet and toast them for about 8 minutes, until fragrant. Let cool, then finely chop the pecans.

3 In a medium bowl, whisk the 2 cups of flour with the baking powder, baking soda, cinnamon and salt. In a small bowl, whisk the oil, buttermilk and vanilla. In a large bowl, using a hand mixer, beat the eggs and granulated sugar at high speed until pale, about 5 minutes. Beat in the liquid ingredients, then beat in the dry ingredients just until moistened. Stir in the carrots and pecans.

4 Divide the batter between the pans and bake the cakes for 55 minutes to 1 hour, until springy and golden. Let the cakes cool on a rack for 30 minutes, then unmold them and let cool completely.

5 MAKE THE FROSTING In a large bowl, using a hand mixer, beat the butter and cream cheese at high speed until light, about 5 minutes. Beat in the vanilla, then the confectioners' sugar; beat at low speed until incorporated. Increase the speed to high and beat until light and fluffy, about 3 minutes.

6 Peel off the parchment paper and invert a cake layer onto a plate. Spread with a slightly rounded cup of the frosting. Top with the second cake layer, right side up. Spread the top and sides with the remaining frosting and refrigerate the cake until chilled, about 1 hour. Slice and serve.

CARAMEL LAYER CAKE

SERVES **16 to 20**

TIME **Active 1 hr; Total 1 hr 45 min plus cooling**

CAKE

- **2 sticks unsalted butter,** softened, plus more for greasing
- **4 cups all-purpose flour,** plus more for dusting
- **2 Tbsp. baking powder**
- **2 tsp. kosher salt**
- **½ tsp. baking soda**
- **2½ cups sugar**
- **1 vanilla bean,** split and seeds scraped
- **4 large eggs**
- **3 cups buttermilk**

FROSTING

- **3 sticks unsalted butter**
- **3 cups sugar**
- **1½ cups buttermilk**
- **1 Tbsp. baking soda**
- **1 tsp. pure vanilla extract**

Nashville pastry chef Lisa Donovan's sweet, fudge-like caramel frosting is the key to this outstanding cake, which is adapted from a recipe by the iconic Southern chef Edna Lewis. Be sure to apply the frosting as soon as you're done beating it or it will harden.

1 MAKE THE CAKE Preheat the oven to 350°. Butter and flour two 10-inch round cake pans and line the bottoms with parchment paper. In a large bowl, whisk the 4 cups of flour with the baking powder, salt and baking soda. In the bowl of a stand mixer fitted with the paddle, beat the 2 sticks of butter with the sugar and vanilla seeds at medium speed until light and fluffy, 3 minutes. Beat in the eggs 1 at a time until incorporated, then beat until very pale and billowy, 3 minutes. At low speed, alternately beat in the dry ingredients and buttermilk until just combined.

2 Divide the batter between the prepared pans and bake for about 35 minutes, until the cakes are golden and a toothpick inserted in the centers comes out clean. Transfer to a rack; let cool in the pans for 30 minutes. Unmold the cakes, peel off the parchment and let cool. Place 1 cake layer on a cake stand or serving platter.

3 MAKE THE FROSTING In a large, heavy-bottomed saucepan, melt the butter over moderately high heat. Stir in the sugar, buttermilk and baking soda. Cook, stirring constantly, until the mixture foams up, then subsides, 5 to 7 minutes. Continue cooking, stirring steadily, until the caramel mixture is very dark brown and reaches 240° on a candy thermometer, about 10 minutes. Carefully pour the mixture into the bowl of a stand mixer fitted with the paddle, add the vanilla and beat at low speed for 3 minutes, until thickened but still pourable.

4 Using a rubber spatula and working quickly, scrape about 1 cup of the frosting onto the cake layer on the stand and spread it to the edge. Top with the second cake layer. Pour the remaining frosting on top. Using an offset spatula, quickly spread the frosting over and around the cake to cover it completely. Let the frosting cool for at least 2 hours before serving.

MAKE AHEAD

The unfrosted cakes can be stored in plastic wrap at room temperature for up to 2 days. Once frosted, the cake can be refrigerated, covered, for up to 5 days.

LEMON-GLAZED CITRUS-YOGURT POUND CAKE

MAKES One 9½-inch loaf

TIME Active 20 min;
Total 2 hr

CAKE

- 1 stick unsalted butter, softened, plus more for greasing
- 2 cups cake flour, plus more for dusting
- 1 tsp. baking powder
- ¾ tsp. baking soda
- ½ tsp. salt
- ¼ cup fresh grapefruit juice
- ½ cup plain whole-milk yogurt
- 1 cup granulated sugar
- 2 large eggs
- 1 tsp. finely grated lemon zest

GLAZE

- 3 Tbsp. fresh lemon juice
- 3 Tbsp. granulated sugar
- ½ cup confectioners' sugar
- 2 Tbsp. unsalted butter, softened

Grapefruit juice in the cake and lemon juice in the glaze give this sweet, tender pound cake from cookbook author Grace Parisi some extra citrus oomph. Be sure to use cake flour rather than all-purpose to ensure a feather-light texture.

1 MAKE THE CAKE Preheat the oven to 350°. Butter and flour a 9½-by-5-inch glass loaf pan. In a medium bowl, whisk the 2 cups of flour with the baking powder, baking soda and salt. In a small bowl, whisk the grapefruit juice with the yogurt. In a medium bowl, using a hand mixer, beat the 1 stick of butter with the granulated sugar at medium-high speed until fluffy. Beat in the eggs and lemon zest. Beat in the dry and wet ingredients in 3 alternating additions; scrape down the bowl as necessary.

2 Scrape the batter into the prepared pan and bake for 50 minutes, until the top is golden and a toothpick inserted in the center comes out with moist crumbs attached. Tent the cake with foil halfway through baking to slow the browning. Transfer to a rack to cool for 20 minutes, then unmold and let cool.

3 MEANWHILE, MAKE THE GLAZE In a small microwave-safe bowl, microwave the lemon juice and granulated sugar at high power for 20 seconds, until the sugar is dissolved. Transfer 2 tablespoons of the lemon syrup to a bowl and whisk in the confectioners' sugar and butter. Using a pastry brush, brush the lemon syrup all over the cake. Allow the syrup to seep in for 10 minutes. Spread the sugar glaze over the cake and let stand until completely dry, about 30 minutes.

"I'm crazy for citrus and have been known to stalk the Test Kitchen during peak season to get my fix. This moist, sweet-tart loaf is a dream. I sometimes make it in mini muffin tins, so each one is like a shot of fresh-squeezed juice." —CHRISTINE QUINLAN, DEPUTY EDITOR

BUTTERMILK BUNDT CAKE
WITH LEMON GLAZE

SERVES **10 to 12**

TIME **Active 30 min; Total 1 hr 45 min plus cooling**

CAKE

- 1½ sticks unsalted butter, at room temperature, plus more for greasing
- 3½ cups all-purpose flour, plus more for dusting
- ¾ tsp. fine salt
- ½ tsp. baking soda
- ¾ cup vegetable shortening, at room temperature
- 2½ cups granulated sugar
- 4 large eggs, at room temperature
- 2 tsp. pure vanilla extract
- 1 cup buttermilk, at room temperature
- 3 Tbsp. fresh lemon juice

GLAZE

- 1 cup confectioners' sugar
- ½ tsp. finely grated lemon zest plus 2½ Tbsp. fresh lemon juice
- 1 tsp. unsalted butter, melted
- Pinch of fine salt

Colleen Cruze Bhatti makes this killer Bundt cake with superfresh buttermilk from her family's dairy farm in Knoxville, Tennessee. It gives the cake a wonderful tang and a soft, tender crumb.

1 MAKE THE CAKE Preheat the oven to 325°. Generously butter a 10-inch Bundt pan and dust with flour. In a medium bowl, whisk the 3½ cups of flour with the salt and baking soda.

2 In a stand mixer fitted with the paddle, beat the 1½ sticks of butter with the shortening at medium-high speed until smooth. Add the granulated sugar and beat until light and fluffy, about 2 minutes. At medium speed, beat in the eggs 1 at a time until just incorporated, then beat in the vanilla; scrape down the sides of the bowl. Beat in the dry ingredients and buttermilk in 3 alternating batches, starting and ending with the dry ingredients. At low speed, beat in the lemon juice.

3 Scrape the batter into the prepared Bundt pan and use an offset spatula to smooth the surface. Bake in the middle of the oven for about 1 hour and 15 minutes, rotating the pan halfway through, until a toothpick inserted in the center of the cake comes out clean. Let the cake cool on a rack for 30 minutes, then turn it out on a platter or cake stand to cool completely.

4 MAKE THE GLAZE In a medium bowl, whisk the confectioners' sugar with the lemon zest, lemon juice, butter and salt until smooth. Drizzle the glaze over the top of the cake, letting it drip down the sides. Let stand for 20 minutes, until the glaze is set. Cut the cake into wedges and serve.

MAKE AHEAD

The glazed cake can be stored in an airtight container for up to 3 days.

APPLE CAKE WITH A TOFFEE CRUST

SERVES **10 to 12**

TIME **Active 1 hr;**
Total 3 hr 45 min

CAKE

- 1 stick unsalted butter, plus more for greasing
- 3 cups all-purpose flour, plus more for dusting
- 1 tsp. salt
- 1 tsp. baking soda
- 1¼ cups vegetable oil
- 2 cups granulated sugar
- 3 large eggs
- 2 large Granny Smith apples— peeled, cored and cut into ½-inch dice
- ¼ cup heavy cream
- 1 cup light brown sugar
- 1 tsp. pure vanilla extract

TOFFEE SAUCE

- 1½ cups granulated sugar
- ¾ cup plus 2 Tbsp. heavy cream
- 2 Tbsp. unsalted butter
- 1 Tbsp. brandy

CARAMELIZED APPLES

- 2 Tbsp. unsalted butter
- 2 Tbsp. light brown sugar
- 3 large Granny Smith apples— peeled, cored and cut into 8 wedges each
- ⅛ tsp. cinnamon
- Vanilla ice cream, for serving

When Vermont pastry chef Lara Atkins was little, her mother made this tube cake for her bridge club; Atkins remembers how she and her brothers would have to wait (and wait and wait) for their slices until all the ladies of the club had served themselves. Atkins now makes the cake for her son, who never has to wait for his piece.

1 MAKE THE CAKE Preheat the oven to 325°. Butter and flour a 9-inch springform tube pan. In a medium bowl, whisk the 3 cups of flour with the salt and baking soda. In a large bowl, whisk the oil with the granulated sugar. Whisk in the eggs 1 at a time. Add the dry ingredients and whisk until smooth. Fold in the diced apples with a rubber spatula. Scrape the batter into the prepared pan and bake in the lower third of the oven until a toothpick inserted in the center of the cake comes out clean, about 1 hour and 15 minutes. Let cool slightly.

2 Meanwhile, in a medium saucepan, combine the 1 stick of butter with the cream and brown sugar; bring to a boil over moderate heat, stirring. Remove the toffee glaze from the heat; stir in the vanilla.

3 Place the warm cake (still in its pan) on a rimmed baking sheet. Pour the hot glaze over the cake and let it seep in, poking the cake lightly with a toothpick. Let cool completely, 2 hours. Invert the cake onto a plate, and invert again onto another plate, right side up.

4 MAKE THE TOFFEE SAUCE In a medium saucepan, combine the granulated sugar and ½ cup of water and bring to a boil over high heat, stirring until the sugar dissolves. Using a moistened pastry brush, wash down any sugar crystals on the sides of the pan. Cook without stirring until a medium-amber caramel forms, about 5 minutes. Remove from the heat and quickly but carefully stir in the cream and butter. Simmer the sauce over moderate heat for 2 minutes, then remove from the heat and stir in the brandy. Pour the toffee sauce into a pitcher.

5 CARAMELIZE THE APPLES In a large skillet, melt the butter and brown sugar. Add the apple wedges and cinnamon and cook over moderately high heat, turning the apples once or twice, until tender and caramelized, about 10 minutes. Add 2 tablespoons of water to dissolve the caramel in the skillet, then transfer the caramelized apples to a plate.

6 Slice the cake and serve with the caramelized apples, toffee sauce and vanilla ice cream.

PREP AHEAD

The unmolded cake can be stored overnight in an airtight container at room temperature. The toffee sauce can be refrigerated for up to 1 week; reheat gently before serving. The apples can be made up to 2 hours ahead and kept at room temperature.

APPLESAUCE–CHOCOLATE CHIP BUNDT CAKE

SERVES **12**

TIME **Active 15 min;**
        Total 2 hr

- 1 stick unsalted butter, melted, plus more for greasing
- 2½ cups all-purpose flour, plus more for dusting
- 1½ cups granulated sugar
- 2 tsp. baking soda
- 2 tsp. cinnamon
- 1 tsp. ground cardamom
- 1 tsp. salt
- ½ tsp. ground cloves
- ½ tsp. black pepper
- 2 cups unsweetened applesauce
- 2 large eggs, lightly beaten
- ½ cup vegetable oil
- One 12-oz. bag semisweet chocolate chips
- Confectioners' sugar, for dusting
- Crème fraîche, for serving

Kristin Donnelly, author of *Modern Potluck,* is devoted to her mother's one-bowl Bundt cake with plenty of cloves and cinnamon. As an exchange student in France, she even paid top dollar for chocolate chips and applesauce at an American market to make it for her host family. Today she adds a kick of black pepper to the batter and serves each slice with a dollop of crème fraîche.

1 Preheat the oven to 350°. Butter and flour a 12-cup Bundt pan. In a large bowl, whisk the 2½ cups of flour with the granulated sugar, baking soda, cinnamon, cardamom, salt, cloves and pepper. Whisk in the applesauce, eggs, oil and melted butter. Fold in the chocolate chips.

2 Scrape the batter into the prepared pan. Bake for 1 hour and 15 minutes, until a toothpick inserted in the center comes out with a few crumbs attached.

3 Transfer the pan to a rack and let the cake cool for 10 minutes, then invert it onto the rack and let cool completely, about 20 minutes. Sift confectioners' sugar over the cake, slice and serve with crème fraîche.

MAKE AHEAD

The cake can be stored in an airtight container for up to 3 days.

"This is an easy, pull-from-the-pantry cake that perfumes your whole house (or tiny apartment) with apple pie spices. Homey and familiar, it's just like the kind of cake Mom would have waiting on the kitchen counter after school."

—JAMES MAIKOWSKI, ART DIRECTOR

CRUMB CAKE WITH PEAR PRESERVES

SERVES **8 to 10**

TIME **Active 30 min; Total 1 hr 30 min plus cooling**

STREUSEL

- **4** Tbsp. unsalted butter, diced, plus more for greasing
- ½ cup packed light brown sugar
- ½ cup all-purpose flour
- **1** tsp. cinnamon
- ½ tsp. kosher salt

CAKE

- **2** cups all-purpose flour
- **2** tsp. baking powder
- **1** tsp. cinnamon
- ¾ tsp. kosher salt
- **1** stick unsalted butter, softened
- **1** cup granulated sugar
- **3** large eggs
- ¾ cup whole milk
- ½ cup pear preserves (4 oz.)
  Confectioners' sugar, for dusting

Pastry chef Stacy Amble makes this streusel-topped crumb cake using Quince & Apple small-batch pear preserves laced with honey and ginger. The preserves are available at specialty food shops and online from quinceandapple.com.

1 MAKE THE STREUSEL Preheat the oven to 350° and butter a 9-inch square metal baking pan. In a medium bowl, mix the brown sugar with the flour, cinnamon and salt. Add the 4 tablespoons of diced butter and, using your fingers, pinch it into the dry ingredients until evenly moistened, then press the mixture into clumps. Refrigerate the streusel until chilled, about 15 minutes.

2 MEANWHILE, MAKE THE CAKE In a medium bowl, whisk the flour with the baking powder, cinnamon and salt. In a large bowl, using a hand mixer, beat the butter with the granulated sugar at medium speed until fluffy, about 2 minutes. Beat in the eggs 1 at a time. Scrape down the sides of the bowl, then beat in the dry ingredients and milk in 3 alternating batches, starting and ending with the dry ingredients, until just incorporated.

3 Scrape the batter into the prepared pan, spreading it in an even layer. Dollop the pear preserves evenly in the batter and sprinkle the streusel evenly on top. Bake for about 50 minutes, until a toothpick inserted in the center of the cake comes out clean. (Some of the streusel will sink into the cake.) Transfer the pan to a rack and let the cake cool completely, about 1 hour. Dust with confectioners' sugar, cut into squares and serve.

MAKE AHEAD

The cake can be covered and stored for up to 3 days.

CARDAMOM-SPICED CRUMB CAKE

SERVES **15**

TIME **Active 30 min; Total 1 hr 30 min plus cooling**

CRUMB TOPPING

- **2** sticks unsalted butter, melted, plus more for greasing
- **2** cups pecans
- **¾** cup light brown sugar
- **½** cup granulated sugar
- **½** tsp. ground cardamom
- **½** tsp. salt
- **2⅔** cups all-purpose flour

CAKE

- **3** cups all-purpose flour
- **1¼** cups granulated sugar
- **1½** tsp. baking powder
- **1** tsp. salt
- **2** large eggs
- **1** cup whole milk
- **1½** sticks unsalted butter, melted
- **2** tsp. pure vanilla extract

GLAZE

- **½** cup confectioners' sugar
- **2** Tbsp. unsalted butter, melted
- **2** tsp. whole milk
- **½** tsp. pure vanilla extract

F&W's Kate Heddings tops this cake with a generous layer of spiced, pecan-studded crumbs, since—let's face it—that's everyone's favorite part. Kate suggests bringing it to a dinner party for hosts to serve at breakfast the next day along with coffee beans and a jar of heavy cream.

1 MAKE THE CRUMB TOPPING Preheat the oven to 350°. Position a rack in the center of the oven. Butter a 9-by-13-inch metal baking pan.

2 Spread the pecans on a rimmed baking sheet and toast for about 8 minutes, until browned. Let cool, then coarsely chop the nuts.

3 In a medium bowl, stir the melted butter with both sugars, the cardamom and salt. Add the flour and stir until clumpy. Stir in the chopped nuts.

4 MAKE THE CAKE In a large bowl, whisk the flour with the granulated sugar, baking powder and salt. In a medium bowl, whisk the eggs with the milk, melted butter and vanilla. Add the egg mixture to the dry ingredients and stir until just combined. Scrape the batter into the prepared pan, smoothing the surface. Scatter the crumbs in large clumps over the cake; the crumb layer will be quite deep.

5 Bake for about 55 minutes, until the crumbs are golden and firm and a tester inserted in the center of the cake comes out clean. If the crumbs brown before the cake is done, cover the cake loosely with foil. Transfer to a rack to cool.

6 MAKE THE GLAZE In a bowl, whisk all of the glaze ingredients together. Drizzle the glaze over the cake; let cool slightly. Serve warm or at room temperature.

"I have a confession: I'm a total crumb-aholic. For me, this cake is the ultimate nutty-buttery-sweet crumb delivery device. In a world of cinnamon crumb cakes, the unexpected hit of cardamom is a nice Scandi-scented surprise."

—JAMES MAIKOWSKI, ART DIRECTOR

MOLASSES-GINGERBREAD CAKE
WITH ORANGE MASCARPONE CREAM

SERVES **9**

TIME **Active 35 min; Total 1 hr 30 min plus 2 hr cooling**

CAKE

Nonstick cooking spray

2¼ cups all-purpose flour

1¾ tsp. ground ginger

1 tsp. cinnamon

1¾ tsp. baking soda

½ tsp. salt

¾ cup plus 2 Tbsp. canola oil

¾ cup plus 2 Tbsp. dark brown sugar

½ cup plus 2 Tbsp. molasses

¼ cup plus 2 Tbsp. honey

2 large eggs

1 tsp. finely grated lemon zest

¾ cup boiling water

ORANGE CONFIT

1 orange, zest removed with a vegetable peeler and sliced lengthwise into ⅛-inch-wide strips

½ cup sugar

ORANGE MASCARPONE CREAM

1 cup mascarpone cheese, at room temperature

¾ cup heavy cream

¾ tsp. finely grated orange zest

2 Tbsp. confectioners' sugar

Pinch of salt

Katie Rosenhouse, owner of Brooklyn's Buttermilk Bakeshop, makes gingerbread year-round, not just at Christmastime. Her ultra-moist cake is excellent on its own and even better with a topping of whipped mascarpone cream and sugary, slightly bitter confited orange peel.

1 MAKE THE CAKE Preheat the oven to 350°. Coat a 9-inch square baking pan with nonstick spray. In a large bowl, combine the flour with the ground ginger, cinnamon, baking soda and salt. In a medium bowl, whisk the canola oil with the brown sugar, molasses, honey, eggs and lemon zest until smooth. Whisk the wet ingredients into the dry ingredients until combined. Whisk in the boiling water.

2 Scrape the batter into the prepared pan and bake for about 1 hour and 10 minutes, until a cake tester inserted in the center of the cake comes out clean. Set the pan on a rack and let the cake cool completely, about 2 hours.

3 MAKE THE ORANGE CONFIT In a medium saucepan, combine the strips of orange zest with the sugar and 4 cups of water. Bring to a boil and cook over high heat until syrupy and the orange zest is soft, about 30 minutes. Using a slotted spoon, transfer the orange confit to a plate; discard the syrup.

4 MAKE THE ORANGE MASCARPONE CREAM In a large bowl, using a hand mixer at medium speed, beat the mascarpone with the cream, orange zest, confectioners' sugar and salt until soft peaks form.

5 Cut the molasses-gingerbread cake into squares and transfer to plates. Dollop the orange mascarpone cream on top, garnish with the orange confit and serve.

PREP AHEAD

The cake can be wrapped in plastic and kept for up to 2 days. The orange confit can be stored in an airtight container for up to 3 days.

PUMPKIN LAYER CAKE WITH
MASCARPONE FROSTING

SERVES **10 to 12**

TIME **Active 50 min;
Total 3 hr**

CAKE

Unsalted butter, for greasing

3 cups **all-purpose flour,
plus more for dusting**

2 Tbsp. **cinnamon**

1½ Tbsp. **ground ginger**

1½ tsp. **baking soda**

1 tsp. **baking powder**

1½ tsp. **kosher salt**

4 large **eggs**

1½ cups **packed light brown sugar**

**One 15-oz. can pure pumpkin
puree**

1 cup **canola oil**

FROSTING

1½ sticks **unsalted butter, softened**

3 cups **confectioners' sugar**

1½ tsp. **pure vanilla extract**

Kosher salt

1½ cups **mascarpone cheese**

This gently spiced pumpkin cake
from F&W's Justin Chapple
features a tangy mascarpone
frosting that beats plain
old buttercream hands down.

1 MAKE THE CAKE Preheat the
oven to 350°. Butter two 9-inch
round cake pans and line the
bottoms with parchment paper.
Butter the paper and dust
with flour, tapping out the excess.

2 In a medium bowl, whisk the
3 cups of flour with the cinnamon,
ginger, baking soda, baking
powder and salt. In a large bowl,
using a hand mixer, beat the eggs
with the brown sugar, pumpkin
and oil at medium-high speed until
blended. At low speed, beat in the
dry ingredients.

3 Scrape the batter into the
prepared pans and bake in the
center of the oven for about
40 minutes, until a toothpick
inserted in the center of
each cake comes out clean. Let
the cakes cool in the pans
for 30 minutes, then invert onto
a rack to cool completely.
Peel off the parchment paper.

4 MEANWHILE, MAKE THE
FROSTING In a large bowl, using
a hand mixer, beat the butter with
the confectioners' sugar, vanilla
and a pinch of salt until smooth.
Add the mascarpone and beat
at high speed just until smooth;
do not overbeat. Refrigerate
the frosting until just set, about
30 minutes.

5 Set 1 cake layer on a platter.
Spread ¾ cup of the frosting on
top and cover with the second
cake layer. Spread a thin layer of
frosting all over the cake and
refrigerate until set, about
15 minutes. Spread the remaining
frosting over the top and sides of
the cake. Refrigerate until firm, at
least 30 minutes, before serving.

MAKE AHEAD

The cake can be refrigerated for
up to 3 days.

STICKY TOFFEE PUDDING CAKE

MAKES **One 10-inch cake**

TIME **Active 45 min;**
      Total 1 hr 30 min

CAKE

Nonstick cooking spray
1½ cups chopped pitted dates
    (9 oz.)
 1 tsp. baking soda
1½ cups all-purpose flour
 1 tsp. baking powder
½ tsp. kosher salt
 4 Tbsp. unsalted butter,
    at room temperature
 1 cup granulated sugar
 2 large eggs
 1 tsp. pure vanilla extract

SAUCE

1¼ cups dark brown sugar
 1 stick unsalted butter, cubed
½ cup heavy cream
 2 tsp. brandy
 1 tsp. pure vanilla extract
½ tsp. kosher salt

Rich and buttery, this riff on British sticky toffee pudding is a "gooey, comforting, warm thing of perfection," says Atlanta pastry chef Abigail Quinn. She drizzles the cake with a brandy-spiked caramel, allowing it to soak up all that amazing flavor.

1 MAKE THE CAKE Preheat the oven to 350°. Coat a 10-inch round cake pan with nonstick spray and line the bottom with parchment paper. In a saucepan, cover the dates with 1 cup of water; bring to a boil. Remove the pan from the heat and whisk in the baking soda; it will foam up. Let cool slightly.

2 In a medium bowl, sift the flour with the baking powder and salt. In a stand mixer fitted with the paddle, beat the butter with the granulated sugar at medium speed until light and fluffy, 1 to 2 minutes. Beat in the eggs and vanilla. In 2 alternating batches, beat in the dry ingredients and the date mixture until just incorporated. Scrape the batter into the prepared pan and bake for 35 to 40 minutes, until a toothpick inserted in the center of the cake comes out clean. Let the cake cool in the pan for 10 minutes.

3 MEANWHILE, MAKE THE SAUCE In a medium saucepan, bring the dark brown sugar, butter and cream to a boil over moderate heat, whisking to dissolve the sugar. Simmer over moderately low heat, whisking, for 2 minutes. Remove from the heat; whisk in the brandy, vanilla and salt. Keep warm.

4 Turn the cake out onto a rack and peel off the parchment. Carefully return the cake, top side down, to the pan. Using a skewer, poke 15 to 20 holes in it. Pour half of the warm sauce over the cake and let stand until absorbed, about 5 minutes. Invert onto a platter and poke another 15 to 20 holes in the top. Pour the remaining sauce over the top. Serve warm.

SERVE WITH

Vanilla ice cream or crème fraîche.

MEXICAN CHOCOLATE CHIP– PUMPKIN SEED CAKE

MAKES **One 9-inch cake**

TIME **Active 10 min; Total 1 hr 10 min**

- 1 **stick unsalted butter, cut into ½-inch pieces and softened, plus more for greasing**
- 1¾ **cups salted roasted pepitas (hulled pumpkin seeds)**
- 1 **cup plus 2 Tbsp. granulated sugar**
- 3 **large eggs, at room temperature**
- 1 **Tbsp. tequila**
- ⅓ **cup all-purpose flour**
- ¼ **tsp. baking powder**
- 3 **oz. Mexican chocolate, finely chopped (about ¾ cup; see Note)**
- 2 **tsp. confectioners' sugar**

NOTE

Mexican chocolate is spiced with cinnamon and vanilla. It's available at specialty food shops and from amazon.com.

For this south-of-the-border take on almond cake, Rick Bayless of Topolobampo in Chicago mixes the batter with ground pepitas (pumpkin seeds), vanilla-scented Mexican chocolate and a hit of tequila. The result: a fluffy texture on the inside plus a delicately crisp crust.

1 Preheat the oven to 350°. Butter a 9-inch round cake pan and line the bottom with parchment paper. Butter the paper. Sprinkle ½ cup of the pumpkin seeds in the pan and dust with 2 tablespoons of the granulated sugar.

2 In a food processor, pulse the remaining 1¼ cups of pumpkin seeds and 1 cup of sugar until the mixture resembles wet sand. Add the eggs, tequila and 1 stick of butter and pulse until smooth. Add the flour and baking powder and pulse just until incorporated. Add the chocolate and pulse until mixed, about 4 pulses.

3 Scrape the batter into the prepared pan and bake in the lower third of the oven for about 50 minutes, until a toothpick inserted in the center of the cake comes out clean; rotate the pan halfway through baking. Let the cake cool in the pan for 10 minutes.

4 Invert the cake onto a plate and peel off the parchment paper. Dust the cake with the confectioners' sugar and serve warm or at room temperature.

VARIATION

For a lighter cake, omit the chocolate and add lime zest.

MAKE AHEAD

The cake can be stored in an airtight container overnight.

GRAPEFRUIT CORNMEAL CAKE

SERVES 12

TIME Active 40 min;
        Total 2 hr 30 min

CAKE

1½ sticks unsalted butter,
    melted and cooled, plus more
    for greasing

1½ cups all-purpose flour

½ cup medium-grind cornmeal

1½ cups granulated sugar

2 tsp. baking powder

½ tsp. kosher salt

3 large eggs

1 Tbsp. finely grated grapefruit
    zest plus ¼ cup fresh grapefruit
    juice

GLAZE

2 cups confectioners' sugar,
    sifted

¼ cup poppy seeds

¼ cup fresh grapefruit juice

New York City–based recipe developer Kay Chun perfumes her cornmeal cake with both grapefruit juice and grapefruit zest. For a striking presentation, she pours on a glaze dotted with poppy seeds.

1 MAKE THE CAKE Preheat the oven to 350°. Butter a 9-inch round cake pan. Line the bottom with parchment and butter the paper.

2 In a medium bowl, whisk the flour with the cornmeal, granulated sugar, baking powder and salt. In another medium bowl, whisk the melted butter with the eggs, grapefruit zest and grapefruit juice. While whisking constantly, add the butter mixture to the flour mixture in a slow, steady stream. Whisk until well blended. Scrape the batter into the prepared pan and bake for about 40 minutes, until golden and a cake tester inserted in the center comes out clean.

3 Transfer the cake to a rack to cool for 10 minutes. Run a sharp paring knife around the edge of the cake, then invert it onto the rack. Peel off the parchment paper. Carefully flip the cake right side up and set the rack over a baking sheet. Let cool until warm, about 30 minutes.

4 MEANWHILE, MAKE THE GLAZE In a medium bowl, mix the confectioners' sugar and poppy seeds. While whisking constantly, slowly drizzle in the grapefruit juice until a smooth, thick glaze forms. Pour the glaze all over the top of the warm cake and spread evenly over the top and sides. Let stand until set, about 30 minutes.

MAKE AHEAD

The cake can be stored in an airtight container for up to 3 days. If there are leftovers, serve wedges for breakfast.

"I don't have a sweet tooth, so this is my kind of dessert. It's light and airy, with a nutty chew from the almond flour. I live for a long weekend brunch that ends with this cake, topped with a mound of berries and dusted with powdered sugar—a showstopper every time." —JULIA HEFFELFINGER, ASSOCIATE FOOD EDITOR

ALMOND CAKE
WITH MIXED BERRIES

MAKES One 9-inch cake

TIME Active 30 min; Total 1 hr 40 min plus cooling

Nonstick baking spray

1 lb. blanched almond flour (2¼ cups)

2 tsp. baking powder

Pinch of kosher salt

1 lb. mixed raspberries, blueberries and strawberries, or pitted fresh cherries

6 large eggs

1 cup granulated sugar

1 tsp. rosewater (optional)

Confectioners' sugar, for dusting

Crème fraîche, for serving

At her cooking school, The Courtyard Kitchen at Dar Namir in Fez, Morocco, Tara Stevens bakes berries into this moist, gluten-free cake, then tops it with even more fruit. It's so popular with her students, who eat it for breakfast, that she usually has to make two a day.

1 Preheat the oven to 325°. Lightly coat a 9-inch springform cake pan with nonstick spray and line the bottom with parchment paper.

2 In a medium bowl, whisk the almond flour with the baking powder and salt. Set aside one-third of the berries in a small bowl for garnish.

3 In a large bowl, using a hand mixer, beat the eggs with the granulated sugar and rosewater, if using, at medium-high speed until very thick and glossy, about 12 minutes. Fold in the almond flour mixture and the remaining berries in 3 alternating batches, ending with the almond flour, just until blended. Scrape the batter into the prepared pan and smooth the surface.

4 Bake the cake until a tester inserted in the center comes out clean, about 55 minutes. Transfer to a rack and let cool for 10 minutes. Unmold the cake, remove the parchment and let cool completely.

5 Top the cake with the reserved berries and dust with confectioners' sugar. Serve with crème fraîche.

PREP AHEAD

The cake can be stored overnight in an airtight container. Top with berries just before serving.

MISO BANANA BREAD

MAKES   One 10-inch loaf

TIME   Active 30 min;
          Total 2 hr plus cooling

1 stick unsalted butter, softened,
   plus more for greasing

1¾ cups all-purpose flour, plus
   more for dusting

5 medium overripe bananas

1 tsp. baking soda

½ tsp. baking powder

¼ tsp. kosher salt

1 cup sugar

¼ cup shiro (white) miso

½ cup buttermilk

2 large eggs

Ken Oringer and Jamie Bissonnette of Little Donkey in Cambridge, Massachusetts, add miso to their addictive banana bread to give it a more robust flavor. The bread is fantastic right after it cools, but it tastes even better the following day—if it lasts that long.

1 Preheat the oven to 350°. Butter and flour a 10-by-5-inch metal loaf pan. In a medium bowl, using a fork, mash 4 of the bananas until chunky. In another medium bowl, whisk the 1¾ cups of flour with the baking soda, baking powder and salt.

2 In the bowl of a stand mixer fitted with the paddle, cream the 1 stick of butter with the sugar and miso at medium speed until fluffy, about 5 minutes. At low speed, slowly add the buttermilk, then beat in the eggs 1 at a time until incorporated. Beat in the mashed bananas; the batter will look curdled. Add the dry ingredients and mix until just blended. Scrape into the prepared pan.

3 Slice the remaining banana lengthwise and arrange the halves on top of the batter side by side, cut side up. Bake for 1½ hours, until a toothpick inserted in the center comes out clean. Let the bread cool on a rack for 30 minutes before turning out to cool completely.

MAKE AHEAD

The banana bread can be wrapped in plastic and kept for up to 3 days.

"I knew this banana bread was a real hit when I brought it to a potluck brunch and a steady stream of strangers asked me for the recipe. They were shocked to find out there's miso in the batter, but every single one of them was still determined to make it." —SUSAN CHOUNG, BOOKS EDITOR

> "Something magical happens to these mini cakes in the oven: The bottom separates into a pudding under a layer of cake. They're also kind of healthy, since they're made with skim milk and loads of fresh lemon." —JUSTIN CHAPPLE, TEST KITCHEN DEPUTY EDITOR

LEMON PUDDING CAKES

SERVES **6**

TIME **Active 20 min;
Total 1 hr 15 min**

Nonstick cooking spray
¾ **cup granulated sugar**
⅓ **cup all-purpose flour**
3 **large eggs, separated**
2 **Tbsp. unsalted butter,
at room temperature**
1 **cup skim milk**
1 **tsp. finely grated lemon zest
plus 5 Tbsp. fresh lemon juice**
¼ **tsp. salt**
**Fresh raspberries or
blackberries, for serving**

These pillowy, vitamin C–packed cakelets, adapted from Sara Kate Gillingham's *Greyston Bakery Cookbook,* are rich without being too heavy. "When you overwhelm dry ingredients with wet ones, the dry ingredients float to the top and you wind up with pudding on the bottom," she says.

1 Preheat the oven to 350°. Lightly coat six 6-ounce ramekins with nonstick spray. In a medium bowl, whisk the sugar with the flour. In another bowl, whisk the egg yolks with the butter until well blended. Whisk in the milk, lemon zest and lemon juice. Pour the lemon mixture into the sugar mixture and whisk until smooth.

2 In a medium bowl, beat the egg whites with the salt until firm peaks form. Gently fold the egg whites into the lemon mixture. Pour the batter into the prepared ramekins and transfer them to a small roasting pan. Place the pan in the oven and pour in enough hot water to reach halfway up the sides of the ramekins.

3 Bake the pudding cakes for 35 minutes, until they are puffy and golden on top. Using tongs, transfer the ramekins to a rack to cool for 20 minutes. Serve the cakes in the ramekins or run a knife around the edge of each cake and unmold them onto plates. Serve warm or at room temperature with berries.

MAKE AHEAD

The lemon pudding cakes can be refrigerated for up to 2 days.

PRALINELLA ICEBOX CAKES

SERVES **10**

TIME **Active 1 hr; Total 2 hr plus overnight setting**

CAKES

- 1 cup pecans (4 oz.)
- 1 stick plus 6 Tbsp. unsalted butter, softened
- ½ cup plus 2 Tbsp. light brown sugar
- ¼ cup plus 2 Tbsp. granulated sugar
- ¾ tsp. pure vanilla extract
- 2 cups all-purpose flour
- 6 Tbsp. unsweetened cocoa powder
- ¾ tsp. kosher salt
- ¼ tsp. baking soda
- 3 Tbsp. whole milk

FILLING

- 2 cups heavy cream
- 1 cup Nutella
- Chopped candied pecans, for garnish (see Note)

NOTE

Candied pecans are available at specialty food shops and from amazon.com.

For these outrageous chocolate and nut icebox cakes, Courtney McBroom of L.A.'s Large Marge catering company layers crisp, baked-from-scratch cookies with a creamy Nutella filling. After leaving the stacks to soften and set overnight, she garnishes them with candied pecans.

1 MAKE THE CAKES Preheat the oven to 350°. Spread the pecans in a pie plate and toast until golden, 8 to 10 minutes. Let cool, then very coarsely chop.

2 In a large bowl, beat the butter with both sugars and the vanilla until fluffy. In a medium bowl, whisk the flour with the cocoa powder, salt and baking soda. Beat the dry ingredients and the milk into the butter mixture in 3 alternating batches; beat in the toasted pecans until just incorporated. On a work surface, divide the dough into 2 pieces. Roll each piece into a 5½-inch log, about 2¼ inches in diameter. Wrap the logs in plastic and refrigerate until firm, 1 hour.

3 Preheat the oven to 325°. Line 2 large baking sheets with parchment paper. Remove 1 log of dough from the plastic. Using a thin knife, cut the log crosswise into ¼-inch-thick slices and arrange on the baking sheets. One log should yield 20 cookies.

4 Bake the cookies for 12 to 15 minutes, until just firm. Let cool for 5 minutes, then transfer to a rack to cool. Let the baking sheets cool, then repeat Steps 3 and 4 with the second log of dough.

5 MAKE THE FILLING In a medium bowl, beat the cream and Nutella until stiff. For each cake stack, set a cookie on a platter and top with 1 tablespoon of the filling. Top with another cookie and another 1 tablespoon of filling. Repeat to make 2 more layers. Repeat with the remaining cookies and filling to make 9 more stacks. Tent the platter with plastic wrap and refrigerate the cakes overnight. Garnish with candied pecans before serving.

MAKE AHEAD

The cakes can be stored in an airtight container for up to 3 days.

FARMER'S CHEESECAKE
WITH STRAWBERRIES

SERVES **8**

TIME **Active 40 min;**
Total 3 hr 15 min

CRUST

5 Tbsp. unsalted butter

3 Tbsp. sugar

1¼ cups packed graham
cracker crumbs (10 to 12
whole crackers)

¼ tsp. salt

Pinch of ground ginger

Pinch of cinnamon

FILLING

1 lb. fresh ricotta cheese,
at room temperature

8 oz. cream cheese,
at room temperature

3 Tbsp. agave nectar

½ tsp. finely grated lemon zest
plus 1 Tbsp. fresh lemon juice

¼ tsp. salt

Pinch of ground ginger

TOPPINGS

1 pint strawberries, hulled and
sliced ¼ inch thick

¼ cup sugar

1 Tbsp. fresh lemon juice

2 tsp. caraway seeds

½ cup honey

San Francisco chef Nicolaus Balla makes his own farmer's cheese (a kind of cottage cheese) for this elegant, no-bake cheesecake. Ricotta mixed with cream cheese is a fabulous substitute for the filling, which is incredibly light, delicately sweet and wonderful atop the crumbly graham cracker crust.

1 MAKE THE CRUST In a small saucepan, melt the butter with the sugar over moderately low heat, stirring, until the sugar dissolves, about 4 minutes. In a medium bowl, mix the graham cracker crumbs with the salt, ginger and cinnamon. Stir in the melted butter until the crumbs are evenly moistened. Press the crumbs evenly over the bottom and up the side of a 9-inch fluted tart pan. Cover with plastic wrap and refrigerate until well chilled, about 1 hour.

2 MAKE THE FILLING In a large bowl, using a hand mixer, beat the ricotta with the cream cheese, agave nectar, lemon zest, lemon juice, salt and ginger just until smooth. Using an offset spatula, spread the filling in the chilled crust. Cover with plastic wrap and refrigerate until well chilled, about 2 hours.

3 MEANWHILE, PREPARE THE TOPPINGS In a medium bowl, toss the strawberries with the sugar and lemon juice. Let stand at room temperature, stirring once or twice, until the berries are juicy and slightly softened, about 30 minutes.

4 In a small saucepan, toast the caraway seeds over moderate heat until fragrant, about 1 minute. Transfer to a mortar and lightly crush the seeds. Return the caraway seeds to the saucepan and add the honey. Warm the honey over moderately low heat for 10 minutes. Strain the honey into a bowl, discarding the seeds; let cool.

5 Cut the cheesecake into wedges, top with the strawberries and caraway honey and serve.

PREP AHEAD

The cheesecake can be refrigerated for up to 2 days. The honey can be stored in an airtight container for up to 1 month.

VANILLA BEAN CHEESECAKE
WITH A WALNUT CRUST

MAKES	One 10-inch cheesecake
TIME	Active 30 min; Total 1 hr 45 min plus overnight chilling

4 Tbsp. unsalted butter, melted, plus more for greasing

1½ cups walnut pieces

1¾ cups sugar

2 cups sour cream

1 Tbsp. pure vanilla extract

32 oz. cream cheese, softened

1 vanilla bean, split and seeds scraped

4 large eggs, at room temperature

¼ tsp. pure almond extract

½ cup heavy cream

This is no ordinary cheesecake. Cookbook author Peggy Cullen bakes hers without the customary water bath, creating a firm yet silky custard, which she tops with sweetened sour cream. Her walnut crust is a wonderful rich counterpoint to the creamy filling.

1 Preheat the oven to 350°. Butter a 10-inch springform pan. In a food processor, pulse the walnuts with ¼ cup of the sugar until finely ground. Add the melted butter; pulse until the mixture resembles moist sand. Press the crumbs into the bottom of the pan. Bake for 12 minutes, until browned around the edge.

2 In a small bowl, mix the sour cream with ¼ cup of the sugar and 1 teaspoon of the vanilla extract. Set aside.

3 Reduce the oven temperature to 300°. In a stand mixer fitted with the paddle or using a hand mixer, beat the cream cheese at low speed with the remaining 1¼ cups of sugar and the vanilla seeds just until combined. Beat in the eggs 1 at a time, scraping down the bowl between additions. Add the remaining 2 teaspoons of vanilla and the almond extract. Slowly beat in the cream until smooth. Pour the cheesecake batter into the pan and bake for 65 to 70 minutes, until lightly golden and slightly jiggly in the center.

4 Immediately pour the sour cream topping over the cheesecake and smooth the surface. Return the cheesecake to the oven and bake for 5 minutes. Transfer to a rack and let cool to room temperature. Run a sharp, thin-bladed knife around the cake and remove the ring. Refrigerate the cake for 3 hours, then cover loosely with plastic wrap and refrigerate overnight before serving.

"Oh my goodness, this cheesecake is such a winner! It's become a staple for so many of us at F&W over the years. It's terrific year-round—perfect with berries in the summer and cranberries in the winter."
—KATE HEDDINGS, EXECUTIVE FOOD EDITOR

SALTED CARAMEL CHEESECAKES

SERVES 6

TIME   Active 30 min;
        Total 4 hr 30 min

CHEESECAKES

- 8 oz. cream cheese, at room temperature
- ½ cup sugar
- 3 large eggs, at room temperature
- ½ cup sour cream

CARAMEL

- 6 Tbsp. light corn syrup
- ½ cup plus 2 Tbsp. sugar
- 3 Tbsp. unsalted butter
- ½ cup heavy cream
- Fleur de sel

Savory-sweet fanatics will rejoice in these luscious, intensely flavored individual cheesecakes from Michael Moorhouse, pastry chef at the Kahala hotel in Honolulu. He coats them with thick, golden caramel seasoned with fleur de sel, then sprinkles on more of the crunchy salt just before serving.

1 MAKE THE CHEESECAKES Preheat the oven to 325°. In a large bowl, beat the cream cheese and sugar at medium speed until smooth. Beat in the eggs 1 at a time, then beat in the sour cream. Pour the batter into six 5-ounce ramekins or custard cups.

2 Set the ramekins in a small pan and place the pan in the center of the oven. Add enough hot water to the pan to reach halfway up the sides of the ramekins. Bake the cheesecakes for 10 minutes, until set at the edges but still quite jiggly in the centers. Turn off the oven and leave the cheesecakes in for 1 hour. Transfer the ramekins to a rack and let cool completely.

3 MEANWHILE, MAKE THE CARAMEL In a heavy medium saucepan, heat the corn syrup. Stir in the sugar and cook over moderately high heat, undisturbed, until a deep amber caramel forms, about 9 minutes. Off the heat, carefully stir in the butter with a long-handled wooden spoon. Stir in the cream in a thin stream. Transfer the caramel to a heatproof pitcher and let cool. Stir in ¾ teaspoon of fleur de sel.

4 Pour 1½ tablespoons of the caramel over each cheesecake and swirl to coat the tops. If the caramel is too thick, warm it in a microwave oven for 10 seconds at a time. Refrigerate the cheesecakes until chilled, at least 3 hours. Sprinkle with fleur de sel just before serving.

MAKE AHEAD

The cheesecakes can be refrigerated for up to 2 days.

TIP

If you see sugar crystals on the sides of the pot while making caramel, dissolve them with a pastry brush that has been dipped in water until it's well moistened.

ICEBOX CHOCOLATE CHEESECAKE

SERVES **8 to 10**

TIME **30 min plus overnight chilling**

70 **Nabisco Famous Chocolate Wafers (from 2 packages)**

24 **oz. cream cheese, at room temperature**

1 **cup chocolate syrup, such as Hershey's**

Cookbook author Grace Parisi brilliantly layers chocolate cookies with a quick mix of cream cheese, chocolate syrup and a little water. The cookies soften as the cake chills overnight for the easiest "cheater's" cheesecake ever.

1 Put 20 of the chocolate cookies (reserving 50 whole ones) into a zippered plastic bag and, using a rolling pin, crush them to fine crumbs. Line an 8-inch round cake pan with enough plastic wrap to extend by 4 inches all around.

2 In a large bowl, using a hand mixer, beat the cream cheese at high speed until fluffy, about 3 minutes. Beat in the chocolate syrup and ¼ cup of water and beat the chocolate cream for 2 minutes.

3 Arrange 9 cookies in an overlapping ring on the bottom of the prepared cake pan and place 1 cookie in the center. Spoon one-fourth of the chocolate cream (about 1¼ cups) over the cookies, being careful not to disturb them. Repeat with the remaining cookies and chocolate cream, ending with a layer of 10 cookies on top.

Fold the plastic wrap over the top of the cake. Lightly tap the pan once or twice on a work surface. Refrigerate the cake for at least 8 hours and preferably overnight.

4 Peel back the plastic wrap and invert the cake onto a serving plate. Carefully peel off the plastic wrap. Press the cookie crumbs onto the sides of the cake to coat evenly. Cut into wedges and serve.

MAKE AHEAD

The plastic-wrapped cake can be refrigerated for up to 3 days.

GLAZED MAPLE–
WALNUT KRINGLE

SERVES **12 to 16**

TIME **Active 2 hr;**
Total 7 hr 30 min

DOUGH

- ½ **cup whole milk**
- **One ¼-oz. package active dry yeast**
- 2 **Tbsp. granulated sugar**
- ½ **cup sour cream**
- 1 **large egg, lightly beaten**
- 1 **Tbsp. pure vanilla extract**
- ½ **tsp. kosher salt**
- 3 **cups all-purpose flour, plus more for dusting**
- **Nonstick cooking spray**
- 2 **sticks unsalted butter, at room temperature**

(continued on opposite page)

"The kringle is an all-out Wisconsin classic," says NYC restaurateur Gabriel Stulman, who went to college in the Badger State. "It's like a giant toaster strudel filled with things like nuts, fruits and cheeses." Here, he and chef Mehdi Brunet-Benkritly flavor the tender sour cream pastry with vanilla, fill it with a walnut mixture sweetened with both brown sugar and maple syrup, then shape it into a giant round.

1 MAKE THE DOUGH In a small saucepan, warm the milk over moderately low heat to 110°. Pour into a large bowl and stir in the yeast and 1 tablespoon of the granulated sugar. Let stand until foamy, 10 minutes. Whisk in the sour cream, egg, vanilla, salt and the remaining 1 tablespoon of granulated sugar. Add all but 2 tablespoons of the flour and stir until a shaggy dough forms.

2 Coat a large bowl with nonstick spray. Scrape the dough out onto a lightly floured surface and knead until very smooth, about 6 minutes. Form into a ball and transfer to the bowl. Cover tightly with plastic wrap and let stand in a warm place until doubled in bulk, 1½ hours.

3 In a bowl, blend the butter with the remaining 2 tablespoons of flour until smooth. Scrape the butter onto a large sheet of plastic wrap, shape it into a 6-inch square and wrap well. Refrigerate until barely firm, about 15 minutes.

4 On a lightly floured surface, roll out the dough to a 10-by-16-inch rectangle. Set the butter square in the center of the dough. Fold the short sides of the dough over the butter to enclose it; pinch the open ends of the packet to seal. Rotate the packet so that one pinched end is facing you. Roll out the dough to a 15-by-8-inch rectangle. (The butter should be pliable; chill the dough for about 10 minutes if the butter is too soft.) Fold one-third of the dough into the center and the other third on top, like you would fold a letter. Turn the dough 90°. Roll out the dough again to a 15-by-8-inch rectangle and fold like a letter again. (This is 2 turns.) Wrap in plastic and refrigerate for 1 hour. Repeat the rolling, folding and chilling 2 more times for a total of 6 turns.

FILLING

1½ cups walnuts

¾ cup all-purpose flour

½ cup packed dark brown sugar

½ cup pure maple syrup

1 stick unsalted butter, at room temperature, plus melted butter for brushing

1 tsp. pure vanilla extract

½ tsp. kosher salt

Turbinado sugar, for sprinkling

GLAZE

2 cups confectioners' sugar

3½ Tbsp. milk

Pinch of salt

📷 PAGE 58

5 MEANWHILE, MAKE THE FILLING Preheat the oven to 350°. On a rimmed baking sheet, toast the nuts for 12 minutes, until golden. Let cool, then finely chop. In a bowl, mix the nuts with the flour and brown sugar. Mix in the maple syrup, 1 stick of butter, vanilla and salt. Cover and refrigerate for 10 minutes. Leave the oven on.

6 On a lightly floured surface, roll out the dough to a 30-by-8-inch rectangle. Spread the filling down the length of the rectangle, leaving a 2-inch border of dough on each side. Fold one long side over the filling, then fold the other long side on top, overlapping by ½ inch; pinch to seal. Slide the dough onto a large sheet of parchment paper and roll it over so it's seam side down. Shape the dough into a ring: Moisten the inside of one end with water and place the other end inside, pinching to seal. Slide the parchment and kringle onto a rimmed baking sheet. Refrigerate until chilled, 30 minutes.

7 Brush the kringle all over with melted butter and sprinkle with turbinado sugar. Bake the kringle in the center of the oven for about 50 minutes, until puffed and golden; some of the filling may seep out. Let the kringle cool for 30 minutes.

8 MAKE THE GLAZE In a medium bowl, whisk all of the ingredients together until smooth. Drizzle the glaze over the kringle and let stand for 15 minutes before cutting into wedges and serving.

MAKE AHEAD

The glazed kringle can be stored between sheets of wax paper in an airtight container for up to 2 days.

"I grew up in the Midwest, and this old-school kringle is pure nostalgia. On my family's drives up north to our cabin, every bakery or market had their own version of this buttery pastry. The key is to keep your dough very cold. Chilled butter yields those dreamy flaky layers." —JULIA HEFFELFINGER, ASSOCIATE FOOD EDITOR

Glazed Maple-Walnut Kringle, p. 56

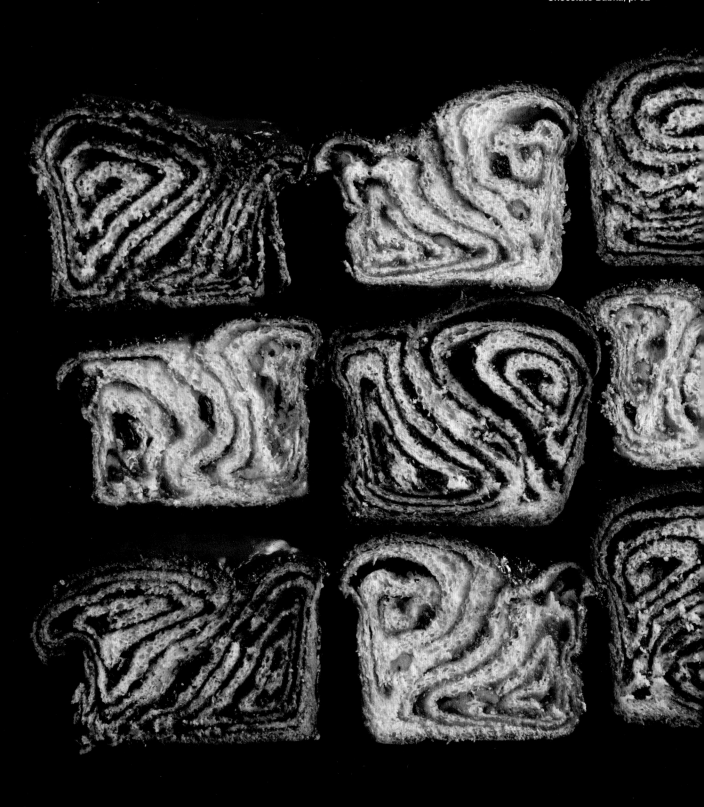

Raisin-Walnut Babka, p. 60, and
Chocolate Babka, p. 62

RAISIN-WALNUT BABKA

MAKES Two 9-inch babkas

TIME Active 1 hr 30 min;
Total 6 hr plus overnight
resting

DOUGH

- **4 cups all-purpose flour,
  preferably King Arthur**
- **⅓ cup plus 2 Tbsp. granulated
  sugar**
- **2 tsp. fine sea salt**
- **1 cup whole milk, warmed**
- **1 packet dry active yeast**
- **1 large egg plus 1 large egg yolk**
- **1 stick plus 2 Tbsp. unsalted
  butter, cut into tablespoons,
  at room temperature**
- **Nonstick baking spray**

FILLING

- **3 cups golden raisins, soaked
  in warm water for 10 minutes
  and drained**
- **¾ cup granulated sugar**
- **6 Tbsp. unsalted butter, softened**
- **1 Tbsp. cinnamon**
- **1½ tsp. fine sea salt**
- **½ cup dark raisins, soaked
  in warm water for 10 minutes
  and drained**
- **¾ cup walnuts, toasted and
  coarsely chopped**

GLAZE

- **1 stick unsalted butter**
- **6 Tbsp. whole milk**
- **2 Tbsp. cinnamon**
- **¼ tsp. fine sea salt**
- **1½ cups confectioners' sugar**

Melissa Weller of Sadelle's in New York City swirls this light and buttery babka with a filling of dark raisins and walnuts and tops it with a luscious cinnamon glaze.

1 MAKE THE DOUGH In a medium bowl, whisk the flour with the granulated sugar and salt. In a stand mixer fitted with the dough hook, combine the milk with the yeast and let stand until foamy, about 5 minutes. Add the egg and egg yolk and sprinkle the dry ingredients on top. Mix at low speed for 2 minutes. Scrape down the sides of the bowl and mix at medium speed until all of the dry ingredients are incorporated and the dough is smooth, about 5 minutes. Add all of the butter at once and mix at low speed until it is fully incorporated and a tacky dough forms, 3 minutes; scrape down the bowl as needed during mixing. Cover the bowl with plastic wrap and let the dough stand at room temperature for 1 hour.

2 Line a large baking sheet with parchment paper and coat the paper generously with nonstick spray. Scrape the dough out onto the parchment and cut the dough in half. Pat each piece into a neat square. Cover with plastic wrap and refrigerate overnight.

3 MAKE THE FILLING Combine all of the ingredients except the dark raisins and walnuts in a food processor and puree until smooth.

4 Coat two 9-by-4-inch loaf pans with nonstick spray and line with parchment paper, allowing 2 inches of overhang on each of the long sides. Roll out each square of dough to a 16-inch square. Using an offset spatula, spread all but ½ cup of the puree in an even layer over the dough squares to within ½ inch of the edges. Sprinkle the dough evenly with the dark raisins and toasted walnuts. Starting at the edge nearest you, tightly roll up each dough square jelly roll–style into a tight log.

5 Using a sharp knife, cut the logs in half crosswise. Using an offset spatula, spread ¼ cup of the reserved filling on the top and sides of 2 of the halves. Set the other halves on top in the opposite direction to form a cross. Twist to form spirals and transfer to the prepared pans. Cover the loaves with a towel and let stand in a warm place until doubled in bulk, about 2 hours.

6 Preheat the oven to 375°. Bake the loaves in the center of the oven for about 45 minutes, until puffed and well browned. Let cool slightly, then use the parchment paper to lift them out of the pans and onto a rack set over a large rimmed baking sheet. Discard the paper.

7 MAKE THE GLAZE In a small saucepan, melt the butter in the milk. Whisk in the remaining ingredients. Spread the glaze on the warm babkas and let stand until set, about 30 minutes.

CHOCOLATE BABKA

MAKES **Two 9-inch babkas**

TIME **Active 1 hr 15 min;
Total 6 hr plus overnight
resting**

DOUGH

- 4 **cups all-purpose flour,
preferably King Arthur**
- ⅓ **cup plus 2 Tbsp. sugar**
- 2 **tsp. fine sea salt**
- 1 **cup whole milk, warmed**
- 1 **packet dry active yeast**
- 1 **large egg plus 1 large egg yolk**
- 1 **stick plus 2 Tbsp. unsalted
butter, cut into tablespoons,
at room temperature**

  Nonstick baking spray

FILLING

- 9 **oz. milk chocolate, finely
chopped**
- 3 **oz. bittersweet chocolate,
finely chopped**
- 1½ **sticks unsalted butter, cubed**
- 1½ **cups finely ground chocolate
wafer cookies**
- 3 **Tbsp. honey**

(continued on opposite page)

This amazing babka from NYC
pastry chef Melissa Weller
gets extra chocolate flavor from
cookie crumbs in the swirl.
As a bonus, the tender babka
is topped with a thick, rich
chocolate glaze.

1 In a medium bowl, whisk the flour
with the sugar and salt. In a stand
mixer fitted with the dough hook,
combine the milk with the yeast
and let stand until foamy, about
5 minutes. Add the whole egg
and egg yolk and sprinkle the dry
ingredients on top. Mix at low
speed for 2 minutes. Scrape down
the sides of the bowl and mix at
medium speed until all of the dry
ingredients are incorporated
and the dough is smooth, about
5 minutes. Add all of the butter
at once and mix at low speed until
it is fully incorporated and a tacky
dough forms, about 3 minutes;
scrape down the bowl as needed
during mixing. Cover the bowl with
plastic and let the dough stand at
room temperature for 1 hour.

2 Line a large baking sheet with
parchment paper and coat
the paper generously with nonstick
spray. Scrape the dough out onto
the parchment paper and cut the
dough in half. Pat each piece into
a neat square. Cover with plastic
wrap and refrigerate overnight.

3 MAKE THE FILLING In a large
heatproof bowl set over
a saucepan of simmering water,
melt both chocolates with the
butter, stirring occasionally,
until smooth. Let cool to room
temperature, then stir in
the cookie crumbs and honey.

4 Coat two 9-by-4-inch loaf pans
with nonstick spray and line
with parchment paper, allowing
2 inches of overhang on each
of the long sides. Roll out each
square of dough to a 16-inch
square. Using an offset spatula,
spread all but ½ cup of the filling
in an even layer over the dough
squares to within ½ inch of the
edges. Starting at the edge
nearest you, tightly roll up each
dough square jelly roll–style into
a tight log.

GLAZE

**12 oz. bittersweet chocolate,
  finely chopped**

 **4 oz. milk chocolate, finely
  chopped**

1½ sticks unsalted butter, cubed

 2 Tbsp. light corn syrup

📷 PAGE 59

5 Using a sharp knife, cut the logs in half crosswise. Using an offset spatula, spread ¼ cup of the reserved filling on the top and sides of 2 of the halves. Set the other halves on top in the opposite direction to form a cross. Twist to form spirals and transfer to the prepared loaf pans. Cover the loaves with a towel and let stand in a warm place until doubled in bulk, about 2 hours.

6 Preheat the oven to 375°. Bake the loaves in the center of the oven for about 45 minutes, until puffed and well browned. Let cool slightly, then use the parchment paper to lift the babkas out of the pans and onto a rack set over a baking sheet. Discard the paper.

7 MAKE THE GLAZE In a heatproof bowl set over a saucepan of simmering water, melt both chocolates with the butter; stir until smooth. Stir in the corn syrup. Spread the glaze on top of the warm babkas and let stand until set, about 30 minutes.

MAKE AHEAD

After the glaze has set, the babkas can be stored in an airtight container overnight.

"To be honest, I've never liked babka. I always found it dry—like a mouthful of sugar. But when we tested this recipe, I had it for breakfast, lunch and a snack for a solid week (don't judge me!). The chocolate is the star, so choose a quality brand to make all your efforts worth it." —JULIA HEFFELFINGER, ASSOCIATE FOOD EDITOR

BUTTERSCOTCH STICKY BUNS

MAKES **1 dozen**

TIME **Active 30 min; Total 2 hr**

DOUGH

- ¾ cup whole milk
- 1 Tbsp. plus ½ tsp. active dry yeast
- ½ cup granulated sugar
- 1 stick unsalted butter—6 Tbsp. softened, 2 Tbsp. melted
- 2 large eggs
- 4 cups all-purpose flour, plus more for dusting
- 1 tsp. kosher salt
  Canola oil, for greasing
  Nonstick cooking spray
- 1 cup light brown sugar
- 2 tsp. cinnamon
- 1 cup pecan halves

GLAZE

- ½ cup packed dark brown sugar
- 6 Tbsp. unsalted butter
- 3 Tbsp. Scotch whisky
- 2½ Tbsp. sweetened condensed milk
- 2 Tbsp. crème fraîche
- 1½ tsp. corn syrup
- ¼ tsp. salt
- ⅛ tsp. pure vanilla extract
- ⅛ tsp. baking powder

"Over-the-top, sticky goodness—or, as I like to call it, 'love.'" That's how New York City pastry chef Catherine Schimenti describes the thrilling moment she first dipped a warm bun into a sweet-salty butterscotch sauce she'd flavored with a splash of Scotch. "I adore adding glamour to old-school desserts," she says.

1 MAKE THE DOUGH In a glass measuring cup, heat the milk in the microwave until warm, about 1 minute. In a stand mixer fitted with the paddle, combine the warm milk and the yeast. Add the granulated sugar and the 6 tablespoons of softened butter and mix at medium speed until the butter is broken up, 1 minute. Beat in the eggs 1 at a time. Add the 4 cups of flour and the salt and mix at low speed until incorporated, 2 minutes. Scrape down the sides of the bowl. Increase the speed to medium and mix the dough for 2 minutes longer. Scrape the dough into a lightly oiled bowl, cover with plastic wrap and let stand at room temperature for 30 minutes.

2 Preheat the oven to 325°. Lightly coat a standard 12-cup muffin tin with nonstick spray.

3 On a lightly floured work surface, roll out the dough to a 9-by-24-inch rectangle. In a small bowl, mix the light brown sugar with the cinnamon. Brush the 2 tablespoons of melted butter over the dough and sprinkle with the cinnamon sugar. Beginning at a long edge, roll up the dough as tightly as possible and pinch the seam. Cut the log into twelve 2-inch pieces and set them in the muffin cups cut side up. Cover the pan and let stand in a warm place for 30 minutes.

4 Set the muffin pan on a baking sheet and bake for 25 to 30 minutes, until the buns are golden brown. Spread the pecans in a pie plate and toast for 10 minutes, until fragrant. Let cool, then coarsely chop the nuts.

5 MAKE THE GLAZE In a small saucepan, bring the dark brown sugar, butter, Scotch, condensed milk, crème fraîche, corn syrup and 2 tablespoons of water to a boil. Simmer over moderate heat until thickened slightly, about 2 minutes. Remove from the heat and stir in the salt, vanilla and baking powder.

6 Unmold the buns. Pour the glaze over the hot buns and sprinkle with the toasted pecans. Let stand until the buns have soaked up some of the glaze and are cool enough to eat, about 20 minutes. Serve warm.

SOUR CREAM COFFEE CAKE MUFFINS

MAKES **18**

TIME **Active 30 min;
Total 1 hr 5 min**

- 1 **cup pecans**
- 1 **cup packed dark brown sugar**
- 1½ **tsp. cinnamon**
- 1 **stick plus 2 Tbsp. unsalted butter, softened**
- 1¾ **cups all-purpose flour**
- 1 **tsp. baking powder**
- ½ **tsp. baking soda**
- ½ **tsp. kosher salt**
- 1 **cup granulated sugar**
- 3 **large eggs**
- 1 **cup sour cream**
- 1½ **tsp. pure vanilla extract**

Scott Finley and John Schulman's Two Old Tarts was a super-popular farmers' market stand before becoming a brick-and-mortar café in Andes, New York. It's famous for the sour cream coffee cake sold at the pastry counter; this stellar muffin version maximizes the crumbs-to-cake ratio.

1 Preheat the oven to 400° and line 18 muffin cups with paper or foil liners. Spread the pecans in a pie plate and toast in the oven until fragrant and lightly browned, 8 minutes. Let cool completely.

2 In a food processor, combine the pecans with the brown sugar, cinnamon and 4 tablespoons of the butter and pulse until the pecans are finely ground and the crumb topping resembles wet sand.

3 In a medium bowl, whisk the flour with the baking powder, baking soda and salt. In a large bowl, using a hand mixer, beat the remaining 6 tablespoons of butter with the granulated sugar at medium speed until fluffy, 1 to 2 minutes. Beat in the eggs 1 at a time until incorporated, then beat in the sour cream, vanilla and 2 tablespoons of water. Beat in the dry ingredients.

4 Spoon half of the batter into the prepared muffin cups and sprinkle with one-third of the crumb topping. Top with the remaining batter and sprinkle the remaining crumb topping evenly over the batter. Bake for about 25 minutes, until the tops are browned and a toothpick inserted in the center of a muffin comes out clean. Transfer the muffins to a rack to cool for 10 minutes. Serve warm or at room temperature.

MAKE AHEAD

The muffins can be stored in an airtight container for up to 2 days.

ALMOND, ELDERFLOWER AND LIME TRAVEL CAKES

MAKES	2 dozen mini cakes
TIME	Active 30 min; Total 1 hr 15 min

CAKES

Nonstick cooking spray

10 oz. almond paste, broken into 1-inch pieces (1 cup)

3 large eggs

2½ Tbsp. cornstarch

Pinch of salt

4½ Tbsp. unsalted butter, melted and cooled

1 Tbsp. St-Germain or other elderflower liqueur

ICING

2 cups confectioners' sugar

2½ Tbsp. heavy cream

2½ Tbsp. St-Germain or other elderflower liqueur

1½ tsp. fresh lime juice

½ tsp. finely grated lime zest, plus zest strips for decorating

William Werner of Craftsman and Wolves in San Francisco created these miniature glazed desserts inspired by French *gâteaux de voyage,* or "travel cakes" (small sweets meant for parties, picnics and other events). He calls them "gussied-up pound cakes."

1 MAKE THE CAKES Preheat the oven to 350° and lightly coat 2 mini muffin pans with nonstick spray. In a food processor, pulse the almond paste several times until broken into small pieces; don't overprocess or the paste will become oily. Add the eggs and pulse until smooth. Add the cornstarch and salt and pulse until smooth. Add the butter and St-Germain and pulse until incorporated.

2 Scrape the batter into a small pitcher and pour it into the muffin cups, filling them about two-thirds full. Bake for about 22 minutes, until the cakes are golden, puffed and firm to the touch. Transfer the pans to a rack and let cool for 20 minutes, then invert the cakes onto the rack to cool completely.

3 MAKE THE ICING In a bowl, mix the confectioners' sugar, cream, St-Germain and lime juice. Using a hand mixer, beat at low speed until smooth. Beat in the ½ teaspoon of grated lime zest. Spoon the icing over the cakes, allowing it to drip down the sides. Garnish with lime zest strips before serving.

"These portable little cakes are an almond-lover's dream. They're an alluring combination of adorable (baked in mini muffin pans) and elegant (redolent of elderflower liqueur and fresh lime). They may be small, but they're definitely for adults to enjoy."
—JUSTIN CHAPPLE, TEST KITCHEN DEPUTY EDITOR

LEMON-RICOTTA CUPCAKES
WITH FLUFFY LEMON FROSTING

MAKES	1 dozen
TIME	Active 40 min; Total 3 hr

FROSTING

- 8 oz. cream cheese, at room temperature
- 6 Tbsp. unsalted butter, at room temperature
- 1 Tbsp. finely grated lemon zest, plus more for garnish
- 1/3 cup honey
- 2 tsp. pure vanilla extract
- 1/8 tsp. kosher salt

CUPCAKES

- 2 cups all-purpose flour
- 2 tsp. baking powder
- 1/4 tsp. baking soda
- 1/2 tsp. kosher salt
- 2/3 cup honey
- 1/2 cup fresh ricotta cheese
- 1/2 cup vegetable oil
- 2 Tbsp. finely grated lemon zest
- 1 Tbsp. pure vanilla extract
- 2 large eggs plus 1 large egg yolk
- 3/4 cup crème fraîche

Joanne Chang, the pastry genius behind Boston's Flour bakeries, makes the perfect grown-up cupcake: lemony, fresh-tasting and sweetened with honey instead of refined sugar.

1 MAKE THE FROSTING In a medium bowl, using a hand mixer, beat the cream cheese at medium speed until light and creamy, about 3 minutes. Scrape down the sides of the bowl. Add the butter and 1 tablespoon of lemon zest and beat until incorporated. Beat in the honey, vanilla and salt. Cover and refrigerate until firm and spreadable, about 3 hours.

2 MEANWHILE, MAKE THE CUPCAKES Preheat the oven to 350°. Line a 12-cup muffin pan with paper liners. In a medium bowl, whisk the flour with the baking powder, baking soda and salt. In another medium bowl, whisk the honey with the ricotta, vegetable oil, lemon zest and vanilla; whisk in the eggs and egg yolk. Whisk in one-third of the flour mixture just until incorporated, then whisk in half of the crème fraîche until smooth, scraping down the side and bottom of the bowl with a rubber spatula. Fold in the remaining flour mixture in 2 batches, alternating with the remaining crème fraîche, until well incorporated.

3 Spoon the batter into the muffin cups and bake for about 25 minutes, until the cupcakes are lightly golden and a toothpick inserted in the centers comes out clean. Transfer the cupcakes to a wire rack and let cool completely. Frost the cupcakes and garnish with lemon zest.

MAKE AHEAD

The cupcakes can be refrigerated for up to 2 days.

"I prefer savory over sweet, so these cupcakes are just my speed. Unlike the cloying ones I grew up eating, this cheery lemon-yellow number is perfectly salty-sweet. The ricotta keeps the cake extra moist, so making a batch a day or two in advance is no problem." —JULIA HEFFELFINGER, ASSOCIATE FOOD EDITOR

CHOCOLATE-BUTTERMILK SNACK CAKES

MAKES **18**

TIME **Active 1 hr;
Total 2 hr 30 min**

CAKES

Nonstick cooking spray
1 **cup buttermilk**
1 **cup brewed coffee, cooled**
1 **tsp. pure vanilla extract**
2 **cups all-purpose flour**
⅔ **cup unsweetened cocoa powder**
1 **Tbsp. baking soda**
1 **tsp. kosher salt**
1⅓ **cups granulated sugar**
¾ **cup canola oil**
1 **large egg**

FILLING AND FROSTING

¾ **cup mascarpone cheese**
¾ **cup heavy cream**
½ **cup confectioners' sugar**
¾ **tsp. pure vanilla extract**
½ **tsp. instant espresso powder**
Pinch of kosher salt
12 **oz. chopped bittersweet
chocolate, melted
and cooled slightly**
**Assorted sprinkles,
for coating**

"I would love to say that I celebrate Valentine's Day by baking for my husband, but he's not into sweets," says Mindy Segal of Mindy's HotChocolate in Chicago. Instead, she makes cookies and cakes and gives them to her friends in vintage tins. These chocolate-buttermilk cakes with sweet mascarpone filling, a nod to Hostess cupcakes, are a crowd favorite.

1 MAKE THE CAKES Preheat the oven to 350°. Generously coat the cups of three 12-cup muffin tins with nonstick spray. In a small bowl, whisk the buttermilk with the coffee and vanilla. In a medium bowl, sift the flour with the cocoa powder, baking soda and salt.

2 In a large bowl, using a hand mixer, beat the granulated sugar with the oil at medium-high speed until blended; beat in the egg. At low speed, beat in the dry ingredients and the buttermilk mixture in 3 alternating batches. Spoon about 2 tablespoons of batter into each muffin cup.

3 Bake the cakes for about 12 minutes, until risen and a toothpick inserted in the centers comes out clean. Let cool in the pans for 3 to 5 minutes. Carefully invert the cakes onto a parchment paper–lined baking sheet (this will help them flatten slightly). Let cool completely, about 30 minutes.

4 MAKE THE FILLING AND FROSTING In a large bowl, beat the mascarpone, cream, confectioners' sugar, vanilla, espresso and salt at medium speed until smooth and thick.

5 Spread the mascarpone filling onto the flat sides of half the cakes. Top with the remaining 18 cakes, pressing down to spread the filling. Dip one half of each cake in the melted chocolate and coat with sprinkles. Refrigerate until set, at least 1 hour or up to 3 days. Serve the cakes cold.

CHOCOLATE–PEANUT BUTTER SWISS ROLLS

MAKES 1 dozen

TIME Active 1 hr;
Total 3 hr 30 min

CAKE

Nonstick baking spray

2 cups granulated sugar

1 cup all-purpose flour

2 Tbsp. unsweetened cocoa powder

1½ tsp. baking soda

½ tsp. baking powder

¼ tsp. kosher salt

2 large eggs

½ cup whole milk

2 Tbsp. unsalted butter

1 tsp. pure vanilla extract

1 tsp. ground instant espresso

PEANUT BUTTER FILLING

1½ sticks unsalted butter, at room temperature

⅓ cup confectioners' sugar, sifted

½ cup smooth peanut butter

⅛ tsp. kosher salt

1 Tbsp. whole milk

½ tsp. pure vanilla extract

GANACHE

9 oz. bittersweet chocolate, finely chopped

1½ Tbsp. unsalted butter, at room temperature

3 Tbsp. light corn syrup

Pinch of kosher salt

1 cup plus 2 Tbsp. heavy cream

Flaky sea salt or chopped peanuts, for garnish

Fudgy cake, fluffy peanut butter filling and a chocolate ganache coating combine to form these insanely delicious personal-size cakes from pastry chef Tiffany MacIsaac of DC's Buttercream Bakeshop.

1 MAKE THE CAKE Preheat the oven to 325°. Liberally grease a large rimmed baking sheet with nonstick spray. Line the sheet with parchment paper and liberally grease the paper.

2 In a large bowl, sift the granulated sugar, flour, cocoa powder, baking soda, baking powder and salt. In a medium bowl, whisk the eggs with the milk.

3 In a small saucepan, combine the butter, vanilla and espresso powder with ½ cup of water and bring to a simmer, stirring to dissolve the espresso. Drizzle the hot mixture over the dry ingredients. Add the egg mixture and whisk until smooth. Scrape the batter onto the prepared sheet and spread in an even layer. Bake for about 20 minutes, until set and a tester inserted in the center of the cake comes out clean (the cake will look wet). Transfer the sheet to a rack and let cool.

4 MEANWHILE, MAKE THE PEANUT BUTTER FILLING In a medium bowl, using a hand mixer, beat the butter with the confectioners' sugar at medium speed until light, about 2 minutes. Beat in the peanut butter and salt, scraping down the sides of the bowl as necessary. Beat in the milk and vanilla.

5 Line a large baking sheet with parchment paper and generously grease it with nonstick spray. Invert the cooled cake onto the prepared sheet. Peel the parchment paper off the cake; it will be sticky. Cut the cake in half lengthwise, then crosswise. Spread the filling all over the cake pieces, leaving a ¼-inch border all around the sides. Roll up the cakes lengthwise (the parchment will come off easily) to form 4 logs. Refrigerate for 1 hour.

6 MAKE THE GANACHE In a bowl, combine the chocolate, butter, corn syrup and salt. In a small saucepan, bring the cream to a simmer. Pour the hot cream over the chocolate mixture and whisk until smooth. Let cool.

7 Line another large baking sheet with parchment paper. Cut each cake log into 3 equal pieces. Working with 1 piece at a time and using a fork or skewer, dip the logs into the ganache to coat all over, letting the excess drip off. Transfer the cakes to the prepared sheet and sprinkle with flaky salt or peanuts. Freeze until firm, about 1 hour, then serve.

MAKE AHEAD

The cakes can be frozen for up to 2 weeks. Serve cold.

CHOCOLATE GANACHE BREAD PUDDING

SERVES **8**

TIME **Active 1 hr;
Total 1 hr 45 min**

BREAD PUDDING

- 5 oz. bittersweet chocolate, coarsely chopped
- 1¼ cups heavy cream
- 6 Tbsp. unsalted butter, plus more for greasing
- ½ lb. challah, crust removed, bread cut into ¾-inch dice (6 cups)
- 1 cup milk
- ¾ cup granulated sugar
- 6 large egg yolks
- 3 Tbsp. unsweetened Dutch-process cocoa powder
- 2 tsp. pure vanilla extract
- ¼ tsp. salt

PORT CARAMEL SAUCE

- ½ cup plus 2 Tbsp. granulated sugar
- ½ cup light brown sugar
- ⅓ cup plus 1 Tbsp. ruby port
- 1 cup heavy cream
- 1 Tbsp. pure vanilla extract

For her indulgent take on the classic, NYC pastry chef Vicki Wells soaks challah in chocolate cream, bakes it with chocolate ganache, then serves it with a warm port caramel sauce.

1 MAKE THE BREAD PUDDING Preheat the oven to 325°. Put 2 ounces of the bittersweet chocolate in a small heatproof bowl. Heat ¼ cup of the heavy cream in a small saucepan over moderately low heat. Pour the warm cream over the chopped chocolate and let stand for about 5 minutes, then stir until the chocolate ganache is smooth. Let the chocolate ganache stand at room temperature until set.

2 Butter an 11-by-8-inch baking dish. In a small saucepan, melt the 6 tablespoons of butter. In a large bowl, toss the melted butter with the diced challah. Spread the bread on a baking sheet in an even layer and toast for about 15 minutes, until golden brown. Wipe out the bowl.

3 In a small saucepan, combine the remaining 1 cup of heavy cream with the milk and 6 tablespoons of the granulated sugar and bring just to a boil. Remove from the heat. Add the remaining 3 ounces of bittersweet chocolate and let stand for 5 minutes, then whisk until the chocolate is melted.

4 In the bowl used for the bread, whisk the remaining 6 tablespoons of granulated sugar with the egg yolks, cocoa, vanilla and salt until a paste forms. Slowly whisk in the warm chocolate cream until smooth. Strain the custard into a clean bowl. Add the toasted bread and toss to coat. Let stand for 10 minutes, until most of the chocolate cream is absorbed.

5 Pour the bread mixture into the prepared baking dish. Using a large spoon, dollop the chocolate ganache on top. Bake the bread pudding for about 35 minutes, until cooked through. Let stand for 15 minutes.

6 MEANWHILE, MAKE THE SAUCE In a heavy medium saucepan, cook the granulated sugar over moderately high heat, stirring occasionally, until melted. Continue to cook, without stirring, until an amber caramel forms, about 3 minutes. Remove from the heat. Add the light brown sugar and stir until smooth. Return the caramel to the heat and carefully add the port; the caramel will harden slightly. Cook, stirring, until the sugar dissolves. Add the cream and cook, stirring occasionally, until thickened, about 6 minutes. Remove from the heat and stir in the vanilla. Transfer the sauce to a pitcher and serve warm with the bread pudding.

"This utterly decadent, high-low mash-up of traditional bread pudding and Krispy Kreme doughnuts is only improved by the killer espresso whipped cream it's topped with." —RAY ISLE, EXECUTIVE WINE EDITOR

KRISPY KREME BREAD PUDDING
WITH ESPRESSO WHIPPED CREAM

SERVES **8 to 10**

TIME **Active 30 min;
Total 3 hr 30 min**

1½ **dozen glazed doughnuts,
cut into sixths**

1 **quart heavy cream**

2 **cups milk**

10 **large egg yolks plus 2 large
whole eggs**

½ **cup sweetened condensed milk**

Unsalted butter for greasing

½ **cup brewed espresso, chilled**

"This recipe was created over a breakfast of—what else?— Krispy Kremes," says chef Govind Armstrong of Post & Beam in L.A. He uses glazed doughnuts as the base of this over-the-top bread pudding.

1 Preheat the oven to 250°. Line 2 baking sheets with parchment paper. Spread the doughnut pieces on the sheets and bake for about 30 minutes, until dry on the outsides and semifirm in the centers. Raise the oven temperature to 350°.

2 In a large bowl, whisk 2 cups of the cream with the milk, egg yolks, whole eggs and condensed milk. Add the doughnut pieces and let soak until softened, about 1 hour; stir every 15 minutes.

3 Lightly butter a 9-by-13-inch baking dish. Spoon the doughnut mixture into the prepared baking dish and cover with foil. Set the dish in a roasting pan and add enough water to the pan to reach halfway up the side of the baking dish. Bake the bread pudding for 40 minutes. Remove the foil and bake for about 20 minutes longer, until the bread pudding is set.

4 Preheat the broiler. Broil the bread pudding for about 3 minutes, until the top is lightly browned. Let cool for 30 minutes.

5 Meanwhile, in a medium bowl, whip the remaining 2 cups of cream to semisoft peaks. Stir in the espresso. Serve with the warm bread pudding.

CRÊPES SUZETTE

SERVES **6**

TIME **45 min**

CRÊPES

- **2 large eggs**
- **¾ cup all-purpose flour**
- **½ cup milk**
- **⅛ tsp. salt**
- **½ tsp. sugar**
- **⅓ cup cold water**
- **1 Tbsp. canola oil**
- **1 Tbsp. unsalted butter, melted, plus more for the skillet**

ORANGE BUTTER

- **6 Tbsp. unsalted butter, softened, plus more for greasing**
- **¼ cup plus 2 Tbsp. sugar, plus more for sprinkling**
- **1 Tbsp. finely grated orange zest plus ⅓ cup fresh orange juice**
- **¼ cup Grand Marnier**
- **2 Tbsp. Cognac**

While restaurants traditionally make the buttery, orange-flavored sauce for this famous French dessert tableside from start to finish, master chef Jacques Pépin finds it easier to prepare largely in advance. He does, however, flambé the liquor in front of his guests and pours it over the platter of crêpes while it's still flaming.

1 MAKE THE CRÊPES In a medium bowl, whisk the eggs, flour, milk, salt and sugar until smooth; the batter will be thick. Whisk in the water, oil and melted butter.

2 Heat a 6-inch crêpe pan or nonstick skillet and rub with a little butter. Add 2 tablespoons of the batter and tilt the skillet to distribute the batter evenly, pouring any excess batter back into the bowl. Cook over moderately high heat until the edge of the crêpe curls up and starts to brown, 45 seconds. Flip the crêpe and cook for 10 seconds, until a few brown spots appear on the bottom. Tap the crêpe out onto a baking sheet. Repeat with the remaining batter to make 12 crêpes, buttering the skillet a few times as necessary.

3 MAKE THE ORANGE BUTTER In a mini food processor, blend the 6 tablespoons of butter with ¼ cup of the sugar and the orange zest. With the machine on, gradually add the orange juice until incorporated.

4 Preheat the broiler. Butter a large rimmed baking sheet and sprinkle lightly with sugar. Place 2 rounded teaspoons of the orange butter in the center of each crêpe. Fold the crêpes in half and in half again to form triangles; arrange on the prepared baking sheet, pointing them in the same direction and overlapping slightly. Sprinkle with the remaining 2 tablespoons of sugar and broil in the middle of the oven until they begin to caramelize, about 2 minutes. Using a long spatula, transfer the crêpes to a heatproof platter.

5 Meanwhile, in a small saucepan, heat the Grand Marnier and Cognac. Ignite carefully with a long-handled match and pour the flaming mixture over the crêpes. Tilt the platter and, with a spoon, carefully baste the crêpes until the flames subside. Serve right away.

GRILLED CHOCOLATE SANDWICHES
WITH CARAMEL SAUCE

SERVES **6**

TIME **45 min**

DARK CHOCOLATE GANACHE

4½ oz. semisweet chocolate chips (⅔ cup)

4½ oz. 70% dark chocolate, finely chopped (1 cup)

¾ cup heavy cream

¼ cup unsweetened cocoa powder

1 Tbsp. sugar

¼ tsp. kosher salt

CARAMEL SAUCE

1 cup heavy cream

¾ cup sugar

2 tsp. unsalted butter, at room temperature

½ tsp. kosher salt

SANDWICHES

Twelve ¼-inch-thick slices of white country bread

4 Tbsp. unsalted butter, melted

Autumn Martin of Hot Cakes in Seattle is a master of warm desserts. Her grilled chocolate sandwiches are crisp, gooey and deliciously messy, especially when they're dipped in a delectable caramel sauce.

1 MAKE THE GANACHE In a heatproof medium bowl, combine both chocolates. In a medium saucepan with a candy thermometer attached, combine the cream, cocoa powder, sugar and salt. Cook over moderately low heat, whisking frequently, until the mixture is smooth and thick and registers 165° on the thermometer, 3 to 5 minutes. Pour the cream mixture over the chocolate and stir until smooth. Let cool to room temperature.

2 MEANWHILE, MAKE THE CARAMEL SAUCE In a small saucepan, warm the cream. In a medium saucepan, spread the sugar in an even layer. Cook over moderate heat, without stirring, until the sugar starts to melt around the edge, about 3 minutes. Reduce the heat to low and shake the pan to incorporate the dry sugar into the melted sugar. Continue to cook over low heat, swirling the pan frequently, until a light amber caramel forms,

about 3 minutes longer. Slowly drizzle in the warm cream. Cook over moderate heat, whisking occasionally, until the caramel is smooth, about 3 minutes. Whisk in the butter and salt. Transfer the caramel to a small bowl and let cool until warm.

3 MAKE THE SANDWICHES Spread ¼ cup of the ganache onto each of 6 slices of bread. Top with the remaining 6 slices of bread and butter both sides.

4 Heat a large nonstick skillet. Place 3 sandwiches in the skillet and cook over moderate heat until golden and crisp and the ganache is melted, about 2 minutes per side. Transfer the sandwiches to a platter. Repeat with the remaining sandwiches. Serve with the caramel dipping sauce.

PREP AHEAD

The ganache and caramel sauce can be refrigerated separately for up to 3 days. Bring to room temperature before using.

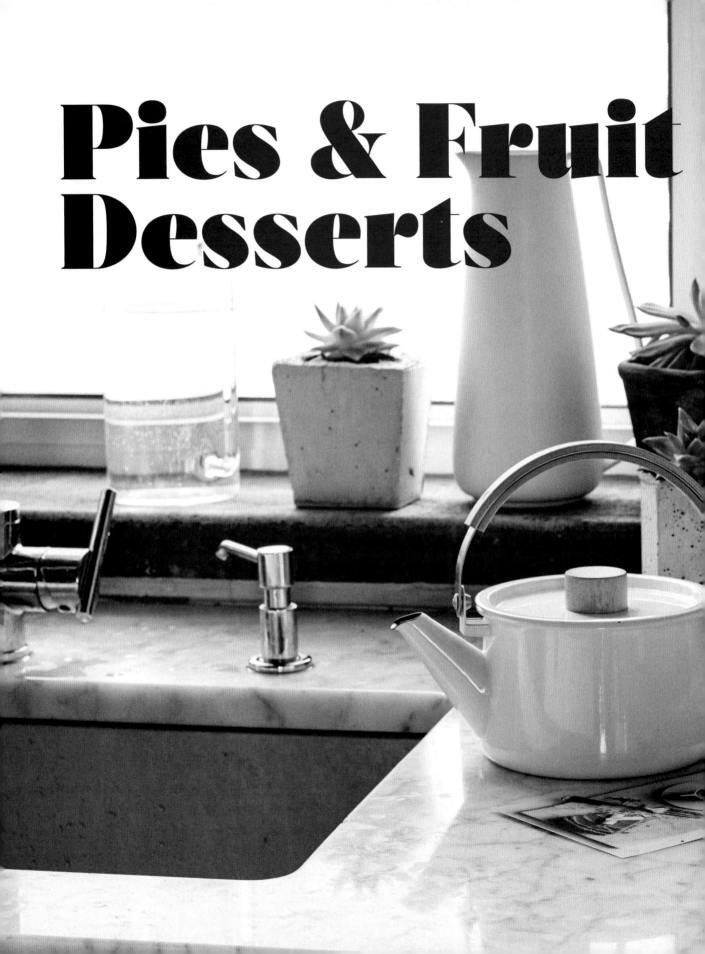

Pies & Fruit Desserts

APPLE CAKE
WITH CRANBERRIES

MAKES One 9-inch cake

TIME Active 20 min;
Total 1 hr 25 min

- 1 Granny Smith apple— peeled, halved, cored and sliced ½ inch thick
- ½ cup fresh or frozen cranberries
- ½ cup light brown sugar
- 2 large eggs
- ¾ cup granulated sugar
- ¾ cup sour cream
- 1 tsp. pure vanilla extract
- 1½ cups all-purpose flour
- 1 stick unsalted butter, melted and cooled slightly
- 1 tsp. baking powder
- ½ tsp. kosher salt

F&W's Justin Chapple makes the most of fall fruit with this easy upside-down cake. He arranges apples and cranberries in the bottom of the pan so that when it's turned over, the fruit creates a beautiful pattern on top of the super-moist sour cream cake.

1 Preheat the oven to 350°. Line the bottom of a 9-inch round cake pan with parchment paper. Arrange the apple slices in the pan in 2 slightly overlapping concentric circles and scatter the cranberries around the edge. Sprinkle the brown sugar on top.

2 In a large bowl, using a hand mixer, beat the eggs with the granulated sugar, sour cream and vanilla until smooth. Beat in the flour, butter, baking powder and salt. Scrape the batter into the cake pan and smooth the surface with a spatula.

3 Bake the cake until a toothpick inserted in the center comes out clean, about 50 minutes. Let cool for 15 minutes, then invert and unmold onto a platter. Cut into wedges and serve warm.

MAKE AHEAD

The cake can be stored in an airtight container for up to 2 days.

MOUNTAIN ROSE APPLE PIE

MAKES One 9-inch deep-dish pie

TIME Active 1 hr 15 min; Total 3 hr 15 min plus cooling

CRUST

1½ cups all-purpose flour, plus more for dusting

1 Tbsp. granulated sugar

½ tsp. kosher salt

1½ sticks unsalted butter, cubed and chilled

¼ cup ice water

2 tsp. distilled white vinegar

TOPPING

1½ cups all-purpose flour

1 cup old-fashioned rolled oats

1 cup packed dark brown sugar

Pinch of kosher salt

2 sticks cold unsalted butter, cubed

FILLING

3 lbs. Mountain Rose or Granny Smith apples—peeled, cored and cut into ⅓-inch-thick wedges

3 Tbsp. all-purpose flour

1½ Tbsp. fresh lemon juice

1½ tsp. cinnamon

½ tsp. ground cloves

½ tsp. freshly grated nutmeg

½ tsp. kosher salt

Rebecca Masson of Houston's Fluff Bake Bar obsesses over the texture of her desserts: "I don't like toothless apple pie," she declares. So she fills her crust with Mountain Rose apples—a super-crisp variety—then tops them with a thick layer of buttery, oaty crumble.

1 MAKE THE CRUST In a food processor, pulse the 1½ cups of flour with the granulated sugar and salt. Add the butter and pulse until the mixture resembles coarse meal with some pea-size pieces remaining. Sprinkle the ice water and vinegar on top and pulse until evenly moistened. Turn the dough out onto a work surface, gather up any crumbs and form into a ball. Flatten into a disk, wrap in plastic and refrigerate until firm, about 1 hour.

2 Preheat the oven to 400°. On a floured work surface, roll out the dough to a 14-inch round, a scant ¼ inch thick. Ease the dough into a 9-inch deep-dish glass pie plate and trim the overhang to 2 inches. Fold the overhanging dough under itself to form a ½-inch-high rim; crimp decoratively. Freeze the crust for 15 minutes.

3 MEANWHILE, MAKE THE TOPPING In a stand mixer fitted with the paddle, mix the flour with the oats, brown sugar and salt at low speed. With the machine at medium speed, gradually beat in the butter. Transfer to a bowl and press into clumps. Cover and refrigerate until firm, about 15 minutes.

4 MAKE THE FILLING In a large bowl, toss the apple wedges with the flour, lemon juice, cinnamon, cloves, nutmeg and salt. Spread the apple mixture in the crust and set the pie on a large rimmed baking sheet. Bake the pie for about 25 minutes, until the crust is just starting to brown.

5 Remove the pie from the oven and gently pack the crumb topping onto the apples. Bake for 30 minutes longer, until the topping is golden and the pie is just starting to bubble. Let the pie cool completely on a rack before serving.

TARTE TATIN

SERVES **8**

TIME **Active 45 min;**
Total 2 hr 15 min

One 14-oz. package all-butter
puff pastry

1 stick unsalted butter

¾ cup sugar

12 Golden Delicious apples—
peeled, halved lengthwise
and cored

Crème fraîche, for serving

Jonathan Waxman of Barbuto
in New York City has tried every
variety of apple and has settled
on Golden Delicious for his
classic tarte tatin; they get
perfectly tender while they bake
but never lose their shape.

1 On a lightly floured work surface,
roll out the puff pastry ⅛ inch
thick. Cut out a 12-inch round,
transfer to a baking sheet and
refrigerate; reserve the pastry
scraps for another use.

2 In a 10-inch cast-iron skillet, melt
the butter. Add the sugar and
cook over moderately low heat,
stirring occasionally, until the
sugar is dissolved and the mixture
comes to a simmer, about
2 minutes. Remove from the heat.
Arrange the apple halves standing
upright in the skillet in 2 snug
concentric circles. Return to the
heat and cook undisturbed
until an amber caramel forms,
about 30 minutes.

3 Preheat the oven to 375°. Top the
apples with the puff pastry and
bake for about 40 minutes, until
the pastry is golden and the
apples are tender. Let the tart
cool for 15 minutes.

4 Place a large plate on top of the
skillet and carefully invert the tart.
Serve warm with crème fraîche.

TIP

If you can't get your apples
to sit up straight in the pan,
Waxman recommends trimming
the bottoms so they lie flat.

BLUEBERRY PIE WITH A RYE CRUST

MAKES   One 9-inch pie

TIME   Active 1 hr; Total 4 hr plus
         5 hr cooling

CRUST

1¼ cups all-purpose flour, plus
   more for dusting

1 cup dark rye flour

1½ tsp. kosher salt

1 stick plus 6 Tbsp. cold unsalted
   butter, cubed

⅔ cup ice water

FILLING

1 vanilla bean, split and seeds
   scraped

¾ cup granulated sugar

½ tsp. kosher salt

2 lbs. blueberries (6 cups)

½ cup all-purpose flour

1 Tbsp. finely grated lemon zest
   plus 2 Tbsp. fresh lemon juice

1 large egg beaten with
   2 tsp. water

   Turbinado sugar, for sprinkling

This sensational blueberry pie from F&W's Justin Chapple has small circles cut out of the tasty rye crust, which not only looks dramatic but also allows moisture to evaporate from the fruit filling as it cooks, concentrating the flavor.

1 MAKE THE CRUST In a food processor, pulse both flours with the salt to mix. Add the butter and pulse until it is the size of small peas. Sprinkle the water over the flour and pulse just until a dough starts to form. Turn the dough out onto a work surface, gather up any crumbs and knead gently until the dough comes together. Cut the dough in half and pat each piece into a disk. Wrap the disks in plastic and refrigerate until well chilled, about 1 hour.

2 On a lightly floured work surface, roll out 1 disk of dough to a 12-inch round. Ease the dough into a 9-inch glass pie plate and trim the overhang to ½ inch. Freeze for 15 minutes.

3 PREPARE THE FILLING In a large bowl, rub the vanilla seeds into the granulated sugar and salt. Add the blueberries, flour, lemon zest and lemon juice and toss well. Scrape the filling into the crust.

4 On a lightly floured work surface, roll out the remaining disk of dough to a 12-inch round. Using three sizes of small round cutters, stamp out decorative holes in the dough, leaving a 2-inch border. Lay the dough over the filling and trim the overhang to ½ inch. Press the overhang together to seal, then fold it under itself. Freeze the pie for 1 hour.

5 Preheat the oven to 375°. Brush the pie with the egg wash and sprinkle with turbinado sugar. Bake until the filling is bubbling and the crust is browned, about 1 hour and 15 minutes; cover the edge of the pie with foil if it browns too quickly. Let the pie cool completely before serving, at least 5 hours or overnight.

FREE-FORM BLUEBERRY TART

SERVES **8**

TIME **Active 30 min; Total 3 hr 30 min plus cooling**

PASTRY

1½ cups all-purpose flour, plus more for dusting

 1 Tbsp. minced candied ginger

¼ tsp. salt

1½ sticks cold unsalted butter, cut into small pieces

¼ cup plus 1 Tbsp. ice water

FILLING

¼ cup sugar, plus more for sprinkling

 2 tsp. finely grated lemon zest

¼ cup all-purpose flour

 4 cups blueberries

 2 Tbsp. fresh lemon juice

 1 egg white, beaten

Jeremy Sewall of Island Creek Oyster Bar in Boston simply shapes the crust for this rustic tart on a baking sheet. He suggests adding a little candied ginger to the crust for a hint of spice; feel free to add more or omit it altogether.

1 MAKE THE PASTRY In a food processor, combine the 1½ cups of flour with the candied ginger and salt and pulse to mix. Add the butter and pulse until it is the size of small peas. Sprinkle on the ice water and pulse just until the pastry starts to come together. Turn the pastry out onto a lightly floured work surface and pat it into a disk. Wrap in plastic and refrigerate until firm, about 2 hours.

2 Line a large baking sheet with parchment paper. On a lightly floured work surface, roll out the pastry to a 14-inch round, about ⅛ inch thick. Fold the pastry in half and transfer it to the prepared baking sheet. Unfold the pastry and refrigerate for 15 minutes.

3 MAKE THE FILLING Preheat the oven to 375°. In a large bowl, mix the ¼ cup of sugar with the lemon zest and flour. Fold in the blueberries and lemon juice and let stand for 15 minutes.

4 Spoon the blueberries in the center of the pastry, leaving a 1½-inch border. Fold the pastry border up and over the blueberries, pleating it as necessary. Brush the egg white on the pastry and sprinkle with sugar. Bake for about 55 minutes, until the pastry is golden brown and the filling starts to bubble. Transfer the baking sheet to a rack and let the tart cool until warm. Cut into wedges and serve warm or at room temperature.

SERVE WITH

Lemon or vanilla ice cream.

PREP AHEAD

The pastry can be refrigerated for up to 2 days.

BLUEBERRY TART
WITH AN OAT FLOUR CRUST

MAKES   One 9-inch tart

TIME   **Active 30 min; Total 5 hr (includes cooling and chilling)**

CRUST

- 6 Tbsp. unsalted butter, softened, plus more for greasing
- ¾ cup oat flour
- 3 Tbsp. white rice flour
- ¼ cup sugar
- ⅛ tsp. salt
- ¹⁄₁₆ tsp. baking soda
- 2 Tbsp. cream cheese, softened
- ½ tsp. pure vanilla extract

FILLING

- 3 cups blueberries
- ¾ cup sugar
- 1 Tbsp. cornstarch
- 1 tsp. finely grated lemon zest
- ⅛ tsp. salt

"The combination of raw and cooked berries is irresistible," says baking guru Alice Medrich about this outstanding gluten-free tart. She has a secret for creating an even crust that bakes up crisp and tender: Press a sheet of plastic wrap against the bottom and up the sides of the dough, then place a paper towel on top. Run the bottom of a straight-sided, flat-bottomed measuring cup along the surface to smooth it out.

1 MAKE THE CRUST Butter a 9-inch fluted tart pan with a removable bottom. In a large bowl, whisk together the oat flour, rice flour, sugar, salt and baking soda. Add the 6 tablespoons of butter, the cream cheese and vanilla; mash and mix with a fork or the back of a large spoon until a smooth, soft dough forms.

2 Press the dough into the tart pan using your fingers or a small offset spatula: Spread the dough evenly all over the bottom of the pan and up the sides. Press a sheet of plastic wrap onto the dough and refrigerate for at least 2 hours and up to 3 days.

3 Preheat the oven to 325°. Set the pan on a baking sheet and bake in the lower third of the oven, rotating once, until the crust is golden brown and has pulled away from the sides of the pan, 30 to 35 minutes. If the crust puffs up too much after 15 to 20 minutes of baking, press it down gently with the back of a fork. The crust can be filled immediately or cooled completely.

4 MAKE THE FILLING Spread 1 cup of the blueberries in the baked crust. In a medium saucepan, combine the remaining 2 cups of blueberries with the sugar, cornstarch, lemon zest, salt and ⅓ cup of water. Bring to a simmer over moderate heat, stirring frequently, about 10 minutes; continue to cook, stirring frequently, until the filling is thick and translucent, about 2 minutes longer. Scrape the blueberry mixture over the raw blueberries in the crust and spread in an even layer. Let cool, then refrigerate until the filling is set, at least 1 hour. Unmold the tart and transfer to a platter. Serve chilled.

STRAWBERRY SLAB PIE

SERVES **6**

TIME **Active 30 min;
Total 3 hr plus 3 hr cooling**

PASTRY

- **2 cups all-purpose flour, plus more for dusting**
- **4 tsp. granulated sugar**
- **1 tsp. kosher salt**
- **2 sticks plus 2 Tbsp. unsalted butter, cut into tablespoons and chilled**
- **2 large egg yolks**
- **¼ cup cold whole milk**
- **Nonstick baking spray**

FILLING

- **1½ lbs. strawberries, hulled and quartered (4 cups)**
- **1 cup granulated sugar**
- **¼ cup cornstarch**
- **½ tsp. finely grated orange zest**
- **¼ tsp. kosher salt**
- **1 large egg, beaten**
- **3 Tbsp. sanding or turbinado sugar**

Joanne Chang of Boston's Flour Bakery + Cafe makes this slab pie in a baking pan. With a flaky crust and a sweet, jammy filling, it's like a giant, juicy Pop-Tart.

1 MAKE THE PASTRY In the bowl of a stand mixer fitted with the paddle, combine the 2 cups of flour with the granulated sugar and salt and mix at low speed. Add the butter and mix at medium speed until almost incorporated, with some pecan-size pieces remaining, about 1 minute. In a small bowl, whisk the egg yolks with the milk. With the machine on, drizzle the egg mixture into the flour mixture and mix until the pastry just starts to come together, about 30 seconds; it will be crumbly.

2 Scrape the pastry onto a lightly floured work surface and gather it together. Using the heel of your hand, smear the pastry against the work surface to work in the butter. Form the pastry into a 1-inch-thick disk, cover in plastic wrap and refrigerate until firm, at least 1 hour.

3 Preheat the oven to 350°. Grease an 8-inch square baking pan with baking spray and line with parchment paper, leaving 3 inches of overhang on all sides.

4 Cut one-third of the pastry off the disk. On a lightly floured surface, using a lightly floured rolling pin, roll out the smaller piece of pastry to an 8-inch square; transfer to a parchment paper–lined baking sheet and refrigerate. Roll out the larger piece of pastry to a 12-inch square, about ¼ inch thick. Ease the pastry into the prepared pan, pressing it into the corners and up the sides; trim the excess pastry, leaving no overhang. Line the pastry with parchment paper and fill with pie weights. Bake for about 30 minutes, until just pale golden and set. Remove the pie weights and parchment paper. Transfer the pan to a rack and let the crust cool completely.

5 MAKE THE FILLING In a medium bowl, toss the strawberries with the granulated sugar, cornstarch, orange zest and salt. Spread the filling in the pastry crust. Cover with the chilled piece of pastry crust, gently pressing it down around the edges. Brush the top with the beaten egg and sprinkle with the sanding sugar. Using a sharp paring knife, make six 2-inch-long slits in the top pastry. Bake for about 50 minutes, until the crust is deep golden. Transfer the pan to a rack to cool, at least 3 hours. Carefully lift the pie out of the pan and transfer to a platter before serving.

DEEP-DISH STRAWBERRY-RHUBARB PIE

MAKES   **One 9½-inch deep-dish pie**

TIME   **Active 50 min; Total 3 hr 20 min plus 5 hr cooling**

DOUGH

2½ cups all-purpose flour

½ tsp. salt

1½ sticks cold unsalted butter, cut into ½-inch dice

¼ cup lard (2 oz.), frozen and cut into ½-inch cubes

½ cup ice water

FILLING

1½ lbs. strawberries, hulled and quartered (5 cups)

1½ lbs. rhubarb, sliced ½ inch thick (5 cups)

1 cup sugar, plus more for sprinkling

¼ cup cornstarch

Pinch of salt

Cookbook author Grace Parisi's strawberry-rhubarb pie strikes the perfect balance of sweet and tart. The dough can be made with just butter, but swapping in some lard yields an even flakier crust. As for the filling, Parisi has experimented with several thickeners, but cornstarch is her favorite.

1 MAKE THE DOUGH In a food processor, pulse the flour with the salt. Add the butter and lard and pulse 5 or 6 times, until they are the size of peas. Drizzle on the ice water and pulse just until the crumbs are moistened.

2 Press the dough into a ball. Divide the dough into 2 pieces, one slightly smaller than the other. Flatten into disks, wrap in plastic and refrigerate until firm, at least 30 minutes.

3 MAKE THE FILLING Preheat the oven to 375° and position a rack in the lower third. In a large bowl, toss the strawberries and rhubarb with the 1 cup of sugar, the cornstarch and the salt.

4 Roll out the larger piece of dough to a 13-inch round, about ⅛ inch thick. Line a 9½-by-1¾-inch glass pie plate with the dough. Brush the overhang with water and spoon in the filling.

5 Roll out the smaller piece of dough to a 12-inch round and lay it over the filling; press the edges together. Trim the overhang to ½ inch, fold it under itself and crimp. Lightly brush the top with water and sprinkle with sugar. Cut a few slits for steam to escape.

6 Bake the pie until the filling is bubbling and the crust is golden brown, about 2 hours. Cover the edge of the pie with foil if it begins to darken. Let cool for 5 hours at room temperature before serving.

STRAWBERRY SHORTCAKE

SERVES **8**

TIME **Active 30 min;
Total 1 hr plus cooling**

1½ sticks cold unsalted butter, cubed, plus more for greasing

2 cups self-rising flour, plus more for dusting

¼ cup sugar

2 cups chilled heavy cream

8 oz. strawberries, quartered (1½ cups)

📷 OPPOSITE PAGE

Cookbook author Ben Mims makes the ultimate shortcake to show off sweet peak-season strawberries. He simply sandwiches the fruit between layers of tender cake and mounds of fluffy whipped cream.

1 Preheat the oven to 425°. Butter and flour an 8-inch round cake pan. In a large bowl, mix the 2 cups of flour with the sugar. Cut or rub in the 1½ sticks of butter until pea-size crumbs form. Using a fork, stir in 1 cup of the cream until a dough forms. Scrape the dough into the prepared pan and lightly press it over the bottom.

2 Bake the cake for 30 minutes, until golden and a toothpick inserted in the center comes out clean. Transfer to a rack and let cool for 10 minutes, then unmold and let cool completely.

3 In a medium bowl, whisk the remaining 1 cup of cream until stiff peaks form. Cut the cake in half horizontally. Spread the bottom cake layer with the strawberries, then the whipped cream. Cover with the top cake layer and serve immediately.

RASPBERRY CLAFOUTIS

SERVES **6**

TIME **Active 20 min; Total 1 hr**

3 Tbsp. unsalted butter, melted, plus more for greasing

½ cup all-purpose flour

¼ cup plus 2 Tbsp. granulated sugar

Pinch of salt

3 large eggs

Finely grated zest of 1 lemon

¼ cup plus 2 Tbsp. milk

1½ pints raspberries (3 cups)

Confectioners' sugar, for dusting

Clafoutis is a rustic French dessert with a texture somewhere between a custard and cake. Alix de Montille of De Montille wines in Burgundy swaps in raspberries for the traditional unpitted cherries, which adds a bit of tang.

1 Preheat the oven to 350°. Butter a 9-inch gratin dish. In a medium bowl, whisk the flour, granulated sugar and salt. Whisk in the eggs, melted butter and lemon zest until smooth. Add the milk and whisk until light and very smooth, about 3 minutes. Pour the batter into the gratin dish and top with the raspberries.

2 Bake the clafoutis for about 30 minutes, until set and golden. Let cool slightly. Dust with confectioners' sugar, cut into wedges and serve.

RASPBERRY-SWIRL
SWEET ROLLS

MAKES **16**

TIME **Active 30 min; Total 4 hr 30 min**

DOUGH

1 **cup milk**
²/₃ **cup granulated sugar**
1½ **Tbsp. active dry yeast**
1 **stick unsalted butter, softened, plus more for greasing**
2 **large eggs**
1 **tsp. finely grated lemon zest**
½ **tsp. fine sea salt**
4¼ **cups all-purpose flour, plus more for dusting**

FILLING

One **10-oz. package IQF (individually quick frozen) raspberries (not thawed; see Note)**
¼ **cup plus 2 Tbsp. granulated sugar**
1 **tsp. cornstarch**

GLAZE

¾ **cup confectioners' sugar**
3 **Tbsp. unsalted butter, melted**
1½ **Tbsp. heavy cream**

NOTE

The rolls are also excellent with IQF blackberries, strawberries, blueberries or chopped sweet cherries (not sour cherries).

Cookbook author Grace Parisi bakes these soft, puffy rolls with individually quick frozen (IQF) raspberries, like the kind sold by Cascadian Farm. In colder months, these clump-free berries are often a superior alternative to fresh fruit shipped to the US.

1 MAKE THE DOUGH In a small saucepan, warm the milk over moderately low heat until it's 95°. Pour the milk into the bowl of a stand mixer fitted with the dough hook and stir in the granulated sugar and yeast. Let stand until foamy, about 5 minutes. Add the stick of softened butter, eggs, lemon zest and sea salt. Add the 4¼ cups of flour and beat at medium speed until a soft dough forms, about 3 minutes. Increase the speed to medium-high and beat until the dough is soft and supple, about 10 minutes longer.

2 Scrape the dough out onto a lightly floured surface and knead it with your hands 2 or 3 times. Form the dough into a ball and transfer it to a lightly buttered bowl. Cover the dough with plastic wrap and let stand in a warm place until doubled in bulk, 1 to 2 hours.

3 Line the bottom of a 9-by-13-inch baking pan with parchment paper, allowing the paper to extend up the short sides. Butter the paper and sides of the pan. Turn the dough out onto a lightly floured work surface and roll it into a 10-by-24-inch rectangle.

4 MAKE THE FILLING In a medium bowl, toss the frozen raspberries with the granulated sugar and cornstarch. Spread the filling evenly over the dough. Tightly roll up the dough to form a 24-inch-long log. Working quickly, cut the log into quarters. Cut each quarter into 4 slices and arrange them in the prepared baking pan, cut side up. Scrape any berries and juice from the work surface into the baking pan between the rolls. Cover the rolls and let them rise in a warm place until they are puffy and have filled the baking pan, about 2 hours.

5 Preheat the oven to 425°. Bake the rolls until they are golden and the berries are bubbling, about 25 minutes. Transfer the pan to a rack to cool for 30 minutes.

6 MEANWHILE, MAKE THE GLAZE In a small bowl, whisk the confectioners' sugar with the butter and cream until the glaze is thick and spreadable.

7 Invert the rolls onto the rack and peel off the parchment. Invert the rolls onto a platter. Dollop glaze over each roll and spread with an offset spatula. Serve warm or at room temperature.

PREP AHEAD

The recipe can be prepared through Step 4 a day ahead. Cover the rolls, refrigerate overnight and then return to room temperature before baking.

DOUGHNUT HOLES
WITH RASPBERRY JAM

SERVES 8

TIME **Active 35 min;
Total 3 hr**

STARTER

- ¾ tsp. active dry yeast
- ¼ cup plus 1 Tbsp. warm water
- ½ cup all-purpose flour

DOUGH

- ¾ tsp. active dry yeast
- 2 Tbsp. milk, warmed
- 1 cup plus 2 Tbsp. flour
- 1 tsp. salt
- 3 large egg yolks
- 2 Tbsp. unsalted butter, melted
- 3 Tbsp. sugar

JAM

- 1 pint red raspberries
(12 oz.)
- 1½ cups sugar, plus more
for coating
  Vegetable oil, for frying

When Ginevra Iverson made these airy, sugared doughnut holes at (the now-shuttered) Restaurant Eloise in Sonoma County, California, she refused to send any imperfect ones into the dining room. Any misshapen holes became snacks for the kitchen crew: "They got slathered with jam and devoured by whoever got to them first."

1 MAKE THE STARTER In a medium bowl, dissolve the yeast in the water. Mix in the flour. Cover with plastic and let rise in a warm place until doubled in bulk, 1 hour.

2 MAKE THE DOUGH In a stand mixer fitted with the dough hook, dissolve the yeast in the milk. Add the flour, salt, egg yolks, butter, sugar and the starter and mix until the dough forms a ball. Scrape the dough into a bowl, cover and let rise in a warm place until doubled in bulk, 1 hour.

3 MEANWHILE, MAKE THE JAM In a saucepan, simmer the raspberries with the 1½ cups of sugar over moderate heat until thickened, about 25 minutes. Scrape the jam into a bowl and let cool for 1 hour.

4 Line a baking sheet with parchment paper. On a floured work surface, roll out the dough ½ inch thick. Stamp out 1-inch round doughnuts as close together as possible. Re-roll the scraps and stamp out more doughnuts. Transfer the rounds to the baking sheet and cover with a damp cloth. Let stand for 15 minutes.

5 Spread sugar in a shallow bowl. In a saucepan, heat 1 inch of oil to 325°. Fry the doughnuts until golden, 2 minutes. Drain, then roll the doughnuts in sugar. Serve hot, with the raspberry jam.

BAKED CURRANT DOUGHNUTS

MAKES **12 doughnuts and 12 holes**

TIME **Active 40 min; Total 4 hr 15 min**

- 1 **cup dried currants**
- 1 **envelope active dry yeast**
  Granulated sugar
- 3 **cups all-purpose flour**
- ¾ **tsp. freshly grated nutmeg**
- ¼ **tsp. cinnamon**
- ¾ **cup milk, warmed**
- 1 **large egg plus 1 large egg yolk**
- 1 **stick unsalted butter, softened, plus 4 Tbsp. melted butter**
- 2 **tsp. kosher salt**
  Canola oil, for greasing

In 1982, Christy Timon opened Clear Flour Bread in Brookline, Massachusetts, hiring Abram Faber to help with deliveries. The now-married couple are revered as early champions of classic European baking. They continue to hunt down rare recipes, like these light, baked-not-fried doughnuts adapted from Robert Jörin, a third-generation Swiss baker at the Culinary Institute of America at Hyde Park, New York.

1 In a medium bowl, cover the currants with hot water and let stand until softened, 20 minutes. Meanwhile, in a small bowl, stir the yeast with 2 tablespoons of warm water and a pinch of sugar and let stand until foamy, 5 minutes.

2 In the bowl of a stand mixer fitted with the dough hook, combine the flour, nutmeg and cinnamon with ¼ cup of sugar. Add the milk, egg, egg yolk and half of the softened butter; beat at low speed for 3 minutes. Beat in the yeast mixture, then add the salt. Beat the dough at medium speed until soft and silky, about 8 minutes; the dough should pull cleanly away from the bowl.

3 With the machine on, add the remaining softened butter to the dough in walnut-size lumps, beating at low speed between additions until incorporated. Drain the currants, pressing out any excess water; beat them into the dough at low speed.

Transfer the dough to a greased bowl, cover and let stand in a warm, draft-free spot until doubled in bulk, 1 hour. Punch it down, re-form into a ball and return to the bowl. Cover and let stand until billowy, 1 hour.

4 Butter 2 large baking sheets. Turn the dough out onto a work surface and cut it into 12 equal pieces. Pinch each piece into a ball and arrange 6 balls on each of the prepared baking sheets, smooth side up. Cover with plastic wrap and let stand for 10 minutes. Using lightly floured hands, press each ball into a flat 4-inch disk. Using a 1¼-inch round cutter, stamp out the centers of each disk and return the holes to the baking sheets. Cover loosely with plastic wrap and let stand for 1 hour, until risen slightly.

5 Preheat the oven to 400° and position racks in the upper and lower thirds. Bake the doughnuts and holes for 25 minutes, shifting the pans from top to bottom and front to back halfway through baking; the doughnuts are done when they are golden and puffy and an instant-read thermometer inserted into the thickest part registers 200°.

6 Spread sugar in a shallow bowl. Brush the hot doughnuts and holes on both sides with the melted butter and dredge them in sugar. Transfer to a platter and serve.

MIXED-BERRY DUTCH BABY

SERVES **6 to 8**

TIME **Active 10 min; Total 35 min**

- 3 **large eggs**
- ½ **tsp. finely grated lemon zest**
- ⅓ **cup granulated sugar**
- **Pinch of salt**
- ⅔ **cup all-purpose flour**
- ⅔ **cup milk**
- 2 **cups raspberries**
- 2 **cups blackberries**
- 4 **Tbsp. unsalted butter**
- **Confectioners' sugar, for dusting**

A Dutch Baby, also known as a German pancake, is a mixture of eggs, flour and milk that gets baked in a heavy skillet until it becomes puffy and golden. In the wonderful version here, cookbook author Grace Parisi folds in fresh berries to create a simple summer dessert that can also double as breakfast.

1 Preheat the oven to 425° and heat a 10-inch cast-iron skillet over moderate heat. In a medium bowl, whisk the eggs with the lemon zest, granulated sugar and salt until combined. Add the flour and milk and whisk until smooth. Add 1 cup each of the raspberries and blackberries.

2 Melt the butter in the skillet and add the batter, spreading the fruit evenly. Bake in the center of the oven for about 22 minutes, until the edge is browned and puffed and the center is lightly browned in spots. Transfer the skillet to a trivet and dust the Dutch Baby with confectioners' sugar. Cut into wedges and serve with the remaining fresh berries.

APPLE-PLUM TARTS
WITH RYE-CORNMEAL CRUST

MAKES **Four 5-inch tarts**

TIME **Active 20 min; Total 1 hr 45 min plus cooling**

DOUGH

- 1 **cup all-purpose flour**
- ¾ **cup rye flour**
- ¼ **cup cornmeal**
- 2 **Tbsp. sugar**
- 1 **tsp. salt**
- 14 **Tbsp. cold unsalted butter, cubed**
- ½ **cup ice water**

FILLING

- 3 **Tbsp. unsalted butter**
- ⅓ **cup plus 2 Tbsp. sugar, plus more for sprinkling**
- ½ **vanilla bean, split and seeds scraped**
- 6 **tart apples (2¾ lbs.), such as Granny Smith—peeled, cored and cut into 20 wedges each**
- **Juice of ½ lemon**
- 4 **red or black plums (¾ lb.), pitted and cut into 16 wedges each**
- 2 **Tbsp. all-purpose flour, plus more for dusting**
- **Crème fraîche or vanilla ice cream, for serving**

Food stylist extraordinaire Susan Spungen puts her own spin on these rustic, free-form fruit tarts by making a super-tender, terrifically tasty crust with rye flour and cornmeal. The recipe is extremely easy on the cook because it can be made ahead at any stage: The dough can be refrigerated for up to three days; the unbaked tarts can be refrigerated overnight; or the whole tarts can be baked and frozen, then reheated shortly before serving.

1 MAKE THE DOUGH In a food processor, pulse both flours with the cornmeal, sugar and salt. Add the butter and pulse until the mixture resembles coarse meal with some pea-size pieces of butter still visible. Sprinkle the ice water over the mixture and pulse until the dough just starts to come together; you should still see small pieces of butter. Scrape the dough out onto a work surface and gather it together. Quarter the dough and form into four ½-inch-thick disks. Wrap the disks in plastic and refrigerate until well chilled, at least 1 hour.

2 MEANWHILE, PREPARE THE FILLING In a large saucepan, melt the butter. Add ⅓ cup of the sugar and the vanilla seeds and cook over moderately high heat, stirring constantly, until the sugar turns light amber, about 1 minute. Add the apples and lemon juice and cook, stirring occasionally, until all of the liquid has evaporated and the apples begin to caramelize, about 11 minutes. Transfer to a bowl to cool, then stir in the plums.

3 Preheat the oven to 400°. On a lightly floured work surface, roll out each disk of dough to a 6-inch round, a scant ¼ inch thick. Transfer the rounds to 2 baking sheets lined with parchment paper. Mix the remaining 2 tablespoons of sugar with the 2 tablespoons of flour and sprinkle evenly in the center of the dough rounds. Spoon the apple-plum filling over the dough, leaving a 1½-inch border. Fold the dough border over the filling, leaving the centers exposed. Lightly brush the tart rims with water and liberally sprinkle them with sugar.

4 Bake the tarts until the crust is browned and the filling is bubbling, about 35 minutes. Let the tarts cool slightly on the baking sheets, then transfer them to a rack and let cool completely, at least 30 minutes. Serve with crème fraîche or vanilla ice cream.

> "I love a recipe that can have multiple iterations, like this one from the amazingly talented pastry chef Megan Garrelts. Another bonus: Your fruit doesn't have to be perfect and beautiful, since it just gets cooked down anyway."
>
> —KATE HEDDINGS, EXECUTIVE FOOD EDITOR

MIXED-FRUIT CORNMEAL COBBLER

SERVES 8

TIME Active 45 min;
Total 2 hr 30 min

CORNMEAL BISCUITS

1¾ cups all-purpose flour, plus more for dusting

¼ cup corn flour

¼ cup fine cornmeal

¼ cup granulated sugar

2 tsp. finely grated lemon zest

1½ tsp. baking powder

⅛ tsp. baking soda

1 tsp. kosher salt

1 stick cold unsalted butter, cubed, plus more for greasing

½ cup plus 2 Tbsp. buttermilk

COBBLER

½ cup honey

½ cup light brown sugar

¼ cup fresh lemon juice

1 Tbsp. cinnamon

½ tsp. kosher salt

⅓ cup cornstarch mixed with ¼ cup water

8 cups raspberries, pitted cherries and sliced plums

Heavy cream, for brushing

2 Tbsp. turbinado sugar

Lemon thyme sprigs, for garnish

Megan Garrelts of Bluestem in Kansas City, Missouri, tops her cobbler with super-light, not-too-sweet cornmeal biscuits. Cut the biscuits in any size rounds, or use a cookie cutter to stamp out fanciful shapes if you prefer. Garrelts uses a mix of raspberries, plums and cherries, but feel free to switch it up to include your favorite mix of fruits instead.

1 MAKE THE BISCUITS In a food processor, combine the 1¾ cups of all-purpose flour with the corn flour, cornmeal, sugar, lemon zest, baking powder, baking soda and salt; pulse to blend. Add the stick of butter and pulse until the mixture resembles coarse meal. With the machine on, drizzle in the buttermilk. Turn the dough out onto a work surface and knead just until it comes together. Pat the dough into a 1-inch-thick disk, wrap in plastic and refrigerate until firm, at least 1 hour.

2 Preheat the oven to 350°. Butter a 3-quart baking dish. On a lightly floured work surface, roll out the dough ½ inch thick. Using a 2-inch biscuit cutter, stamp out rounds, re-rolling the scraps.

3 MAKE THE COBBLER In a large bowl, mix the honey with the brown sugar, lemon juice, cinnamon and salt. Stir and add the cornstarch mixture, then add the fruit and toss gently. Spread the fruit in the prepared dish and top with the biscuits. Brush the biscuits with cream and sprinkle with the turbinado sugar. Bake until the fruit is bubbling and the biscuits are golden, about 45 minutes. Garnish with lemon thyme and serve warm.

SERVE WITH

Whipped cream.

CHERRY JAM-AND-RICOTTA TART

SERVES **8**

TIME **Active 45 min;
Total 2 hr 30 min plus
overnight chilling**

2¼ cups all-purpose flour, plus
  more for dusting

1 stick plus 2 Tbsp. cold unsalted
  butter, cubed, plus more for
  greasing

¾ cup superfine sugar

1 tsp. finely grated
  lemon zest

  Pinch of kosher salt

4 large eggs plus 1 large egg yolk

1 lb. fresh ricotta cheese
  (2 cups)

  One 13-oz. jar cherry or sour
  cherry jam (1¼ cups)

  Whipped cream, for serving

"Romans are masters at using 'the fifth quarter,' things that are usually discarded—like ricotta, a by-product of making pecorino cheese," says Rachel Roddy, a Rome-based blogger and author of *My Kitchen in Rome.* She adds lushness to this spectacular double-crust fruity tart with a thick layer of fresh ricotta.

1 In a medium bowl, combine the 2¼ cups of flour and cubed butter. Using your fingertips, rub the butter into the flour until the mixture resembles fine breadcrumbs. Stir in ½ cup of the sugar, the lemon zest and salt. In a small bowl, beat 2 of the whole eggs; add to the flour mixture and stir with a wooden spoon until a dough starts to come together. Knead with your hands just until a dough forms. Divide the dough into a one-third piece and a two-thirds piece; pat each piece into a 1-inch-thick disk and wrap in plastic. Refrigerate for at least 1 hour or overnight.

2 Preheat the oven to 350°. Lightly butter a 9-inch fluted tart pan. In a small bowl, whisk the ricotta cheese with 1 whole egg, the egg yolk and the remaining ¼ cup of sugar until blended.

3 On a lightly floured surface, using a lightly floured rolling pin, roll out the larger piece of dough to a 12-inch round, about ⅛ inch thick. Ease the dough into the prepared pan and trim off the excess; prick the bottom of the dough all over with a fork. Spread the jam in an even layer over the bottom of the tart and spread the ricotta mixture evenly on top of the jam.

4 Roll out the remaining piece of dough to a 10-inch round. Using a sharp knife, cut the pastry into strips of different widths and arrange on top of the ricotta, leaving space between the strips and pressing them to adhere to the rim of the pan.

5 In a small bowl, beat the remaining egg and brush onto the pastry strips. Bake the tart in the center of the oven for about 50 minutes, until the crust is golden and the filling is set. Transfer to a rack and let cool to room temperature. Cover and refrigerate overnight. Serve chilled, with whipped cream.

MAKE AHEAD

The tart can be refrigerated for up to 2 days.

PLUM GALETTE

SERVES **8**

TIME **Active 30 min;**
     Total 2 hr plus cooling

PÂTE BRISÉE

1½ cups all-purpose flour, plus
   more for dusting

1½ sticks cold unsalted butter,
   cut into ½-inch pieces

¼ tsp. salt

⅓ cup ice water

FILLING

¼ cup plus ⅓ cup sugar

3 Tbsp. ground almonds

3 Tbsp. all-purpose flour

2½ lbs. large plums—halved, pitted
   and cut into ½-inch wedges

3 Tbsp. unsalted butter, cut into
   small bits

½ cup good-quality plum, apricot
   or raspberry preserves,
   strained if chunky or seedy

This galette is a favorite dessert at master chef Jacques Pépin's house. You can make it with any seasonal fruit, such as rhubarb, peaches, cherries, apricots or apples. The dough is buttery, flaky and very forgiving—and it comes together in 10 seconds in a food processor.

1 MAKE THE PÂTE BRISÉE Put the 1½ cups of flour, the butter and salt in a food processor and process for 5 seconds; the butter should still be in pieces. Add the ice water and process for 5 seconds longer, just until the dough comes together; the butter should still be visible.

2 Remove the dough from the processor and gather it into a ball. On a lightly floured surface, roll out the dough to a 16-by-18-inch oval, ¹⁄₁₆ to ⅛ inch thick. Drape the dough over the rolling pin and transfer it to a large, heavy baking sheet. Chill the dough until firm, about 20 minutes. Preheat the oven to 400°.

3 MAKE THE FILLING In a small bowl, combine ¼ cup of the sugar with the ground almonds and flour. Spread this mixture evenly over the dough to within 2 inches of the edge. Arrange the plum wedges on top and dot with the butter. Sprinkle all but 1 teaspoon of the remaining ⅓ cup of sugar over the fruit. Fold the edge of the dough up over the plums to create a 2-inch border. (If the dough feels cold and firm, wait for a few minutes until it softens to prevent it from cracking.) Sprinkle the border with the reserved 1 teaspoon of sugar.

4 Bake the galette in the middle of the oven for about 1 hour, until the fruit is very soft and the crust is richly browned. If any juices have leaked onto the baking sheet, slide a knife under the galette to release it from the sheet. Evenly brush the preserves over the hot fruit; brush some up onto the crust, too, if desired. Let the galette cool to room temperature before serving.

"On those languorous summer days when making a pie seems like too much of a bother, I turn to this rustic, unfussy galette. My favorite lazy-day filling is blueberries. You don't even have to pit or cut them up, and they cook down into a delicious, jammy mess."
—SUSAN CHOUNG, BOOKS EDITOR

SKILLET GRAHAM CAKE
WITH PEACHES AND BLUEBERRIES

SERVES **10**

TIME **Active 1 hr;
Total 3 hr 30 min**

STREUSEL

¾ **cup graham cracker crumbs**

¾ **cup all-purpose flour**

½ **cup light brown sugar**

1 **stick unsalted butter, softened**

½ **tsp. kosher salt**

FRUIT

3 **large peaches, each cut into
1-inch wedges**

¾ **cup blueberries**

½ **cup granulated sugar**

3 **Tbsp. fresh lemon juice**

1 **Tbsp. cornstarch**

1 **Tbsp. unsalted butter**

CAKE

1½ **cups all-purpose flour**

½ **cup whole-wheat flour**

½ **cup fine graham cracker crumbs**

2 **tsp. baking powder**

1½ **tsp. kosher salt**

1 **stick plus 3 Tbsp. unsalted
butter, softened**

1¼ **cups light brown sugar**

¼ **cup granulated sugar**

3 **Tbsp. honey**

4 **large eggs**

1¼ **cups buttermilk**

⅓ **cup canola oil**

1 **Tbsp. pure vanilla extract
Vanilla ice cream, for serving**

For cookouts in her backyard, Stephanie Izard of Girl & the Goat in Chicago makes this cake in a cast-iron skillet set right on the grill. It gets amazing flavor from graham crackers mixed into both the batter and the crumbly streusel topping. The cake can also be baked in a 300° oven.

1 MAKE THE STREUSEL In a stand mixer fitted with the paddle, beat all of the ingredients together at medium speed until crumbs form. Transfer the crumbs to a bowl and press into clumps. Refrigerate until chilled, about 15 minutes.

2 MEANWHILE, PREPARE THE FRUIT Set up a gas grill for indirect grilling, then heat to 300°. In a medium bowl, toss the peaches with the blueberries, granulated sugar, lemon juice and cornstarch. In a 12-inch cast-iron skillet, melt the butter over low heat. Remove from the heat. Scrape the fruit and any juices into the skillet.

3 MAKE THE CAKE In a medium bowl, whisk both flours with the graham cracker crumbs, baking powder and salt. In a stand mixer fitted with the paddle, beat the butter with both sugars and the honey at medium speed until fluffy. Beat in the eggs 1 at a time, then beat in the buttermilk, oil and vanilla. Scrape down the bowl and beat in the dry ingredients until just smooth. Spread the batter in the skillet in an even layer. Scatter the streusel evenly on top.

4 Set the skillet on the grill over indirect heat. Close the grill and bake for about 1½ hours, rotating the skillet every 20 minutes, until a toothpick inserted in the cake comes out clean; keep an eye on the heat to maintain the grill temperature. Let the cake cool for 1 hour. Cut into wedges and serve with vanilla ice cream.

INGREDIENT TIP

When choosing fruit that you plan to grill or bake, always be sure that it's perfectly ripe but still on the firm side.

POACHED PEACHES
WITH BAKED RICOTTA

SERVES **8 to 10**

TIME **Active 30 min; Total 1 hr 15 min plus 3 hr cooling**

BAKED RICOTTA

Nonstick baking spray

2¼ **lbs. fresh ricotta cheese (4½ cups)**

2 **vanilla beans, split and seeds scraped**

1½ **Tbsp. finely grated lemon zest**

9 **large eggs**

¾ **cup sugar**

¼ **cup plus 2 Tbsp. all-purpose flour**

½ **tsp. kosher salt**

PEACHES

1 **cup sugar**

½ **cup honey**

3 **fresh lemon verbena sprigs or 1 cup loosely packed dried leaves, plus additional fresh sprigs for garnish (optional)**

10 **ripe but firm peaches (about 4½ lbs.), halved and pitted**

"In hot weather, I like the idea of a simple fruit dessert," says *Top Chef* head judge Tom Colicchio. For a lovely, light finish to a summer meal, he serves peaches poached in lemon verbena–infused syrup with squares of creamy baked ricotta.

1 MAKE THE BAKED RICOTTA Preheat the oven to 350°. Lightly coat a 2½-quart glass or ceramic baking dish with baking spray and set the dish in a roasting pan.

2 In a colander set over a large bowl, drain the ricotta, gently pressing out any excess liquid; discard the liquid. Transfer the ricotta to a large bowl and stir in the vanilla seeds and lemon zest.

3 In another large bowl, whisk the eggs and sugar until smooth. Whisk the egg mixture into the ricotta until smooth, then fold in the flour and salt. Pour the mixture into the baking dish. Add enough hot water to the roasting pan to reach halfway up the side of the baking dish. Bake the ricotta for about 40 minutes, until lightly golden on top and just set in the center. Transfer the dish to a rack and let cool to room temperature, about 3 hours.

4 MEANWHILE, PREPARE THE PEACHES In a large saucepan, combine the sugar, honey and 4 cups of water and bring to a simmer. If using dried lemon verbena, wrap the leaves in a large square of cheesecloth and tie with kitchen string. Add the lemon verbena and peaches to the saucepan. Bring just to a boil, then simmer gently over moderately low heat, turning the peaches occasionally, until just tender, 7 to 8 minutes. Using a slotted spoon, transfer the peaches to a baking sheet. Let cool slightly, then slip off the skins.

5 Discard the lemon verbena and simmer the poaching liquid over moderate heat until reduced to a light syrup, about 10 minutes. Strain the syrup into a bowl and let cool to room temperature, about 1 hour.

6 Cut the baked ricotta into squares and serve with the poached peaches and syrup. Garnish with lemon verbena sprigs.

PEACH HAND PIES

MAKES **16**

TIME **Active 1 hr; Total 4 hr**

FILLING

- **3 small peaches (about 12 oz.)**
- **¼ cup granulated sugar**
- **¼ cup light brown sugar**
- **¼ tsp. kosher salt**
- **¼ tsp. cinnamon**
- **1 tsp. finely grated lemon zest plus 1 Tbsp. fresh lemon juice**
- **½ vanilla bean, split and seeds scraped, pod reserved for another use**

DOUGH

- **2½ cups all-purpose flour, plus more for dusting**
- **1 tsp. kosher salt**
- **2 sticks cold unsalted butter, cubed**
- **½ cup ice water**
- **1 large egg, lightly beaten**
- **Turbinado sugar, for sprinkling**

Lisa Donovan makes these adorable peach pies for her Nashville-based online bakery, Buttermilk Road. A fun alternative to a traditional pie, they can be frozen up to a month in advance and popped in the oven for an impressive last-minute dessert.

1 MAKE THE FILLING Bring a medium saucepan of water to a boil. Fill a bowl with ice water. Using a sharp paring knife, mark an X on the bottom of each peach. Add the peaches to the saucepan and blanch until the skins start to peel away, 1 to 2 minutes. Transfer to the ice bath and let cool completely. Peel, halve and pit the peaches and cut into ¼-inch pieces; you should have about 2 cups. Wipe out the saucepan.

2 In the same saucepan, combine the peaches with all the remaining ingredients and bring to a boil. Cook over moderate heat, stirring occasionally, until thickened and syrupy, about 12 minutes. Scrape the filling into a small bowl; let cool to room temperature. Cover and refrigerate until cold, 2 hours.

3 MEANWHILE, MAKE THE DOUGH In a large bowl, whisk the 2½ cups of flour with the salt. Scatter the butter over the flour and pinch it in with your fingers until the mixture resembles very coarse crumbs, with some pieces the size of small peas. Stir in the ice water just until a dough forms. Turn out onto a lightly floured work surface and knead gently to form a ball. Pat into a 1-inch-thick round, wrap in plastic and refrigerate for 1 hour.

4 Preheat the oven to 450° and line a baking sheet with parchment paper. Cut the dough in half. On a lightly floured work surface, using a lightly floured rolling pin, roll out 1 piece of dough ⅛ inch thick. Using a 4-inch biscuit cutter, stamp out 6 rounds and transfer to the prepared baking sheet. Gather the scraps and form into a ball; roll out again and stamp out 2 more rounds. Transfer to the baking sheet. Top with parchment paper. Repeat with the second piece of dough, placing 8 rounds on the parchment. Refrigerate for 30 minutes.

5 Line 2 baking sheets with parchment paper. Working with 1 dough round at a time, brush the rim with the beaten egg. Spoon 2 teaspoons of the filling into the center and fold the round in half to enclose. Press the edge firmly to seal and transfer to a prepared baking sheet. Repeat with the remaining dough and filling, arranging the hand pies 2 inches apart on the sheets. Brush the tops with the remaining beaten egg and sprinkle with turbinado sugar. Using a paring knife, cut 2 or 3 small slits in each hand pie. Bake until puffed and golden brown, shifting the pans from top to bottom and back to front halfway through, about 18 minutes. Transfer the hand pies to a rack and let cool slightly before serving.

TANGERINE CURD TART

SERVES **8**

TIME **Active 1 hr 30 min; Total 3 hr 30 min plus 3 hr chilling**

TART SHELL

- 1½ **cups all-purpose flour, plus more for dusting**
- ½ **tsp. granulated sugar**
- ½ **tsp. kosher salt**
- 1 **stick unsalted butter, cubed and chilled**
- ¼ **cup ice water**

TANGERINE CURD

- 2 **tsp. finely grated tangerine zest plus 1 cup freshly squeezed tangerine juice (not bottled)**
- 5 **Tbsp. fresh lemon juice**
- 1 **cup granulated sugar**
- 12 **large egg yolks**
  Pinch of kosher salt
- 1½ **sticks unsalted butter, cubed and at room temperature**

WHIPPED CREAM

- 1 **cup heavy cream**
- 2 **tsp. confectioners' sugar**

NYC-based recipe developer Kay Chun bakes this beautiful, sunny-yellow tart for special occasions. Fresh tangerine and lemon juices make it a standout.

1 MAKE THE TART SHELL In a small bowl, whisk the 1½ cups of flour, granulated sugar and salt. Add the butter and blend it in with your fingertips until pea-size pieces remain. Stir in the ice water until the dough comes together; add another tablespoon if the dough seems too dry. Turn the dough out onto a lightly floured surface and pat into a 1-inch-thick disk. Wrap in plastic; refrigerate for 1 hour.

2 On a lightly floured work surface, roll out the dough to an 8-by-18-inch rectangle, about ⅛ inch thick. Fit the dough into a 13-by-4-inch fluted tart pan with a removable bottom. Trim the overhang. Cover with plastic wrap and freeze for 30 minutes.

3 Preheat the oven to 400°. Line the tart shell with parchment paper and fill with pie weights. Bake for 40 minutes, until set. Remove the paper and pie weights and bake for 10 minutes, until cooked through. Transfer to a rack and let cool completely.

4 MEANWHILE, MAKE THE TANGERINE CURD In a medium saucepan, whisk the tangerine zest with the citrus juices, granulated sugar, egg yolks and salt. Cook over moderately low heat, stirring often with a spatula, until the curd is very thick but pourable, about 30 minutes. Strain through a fine sieve into a medium bowl and whisk in the butter. Scrape the curd into the tart shell and press a sheet of plastic wrap directly onto the surface. Refrigerate until set and chilled, at least 3 hours.

5 MAKE THE WHIPPED CREAM In a medium bowl, beat the cream with the confectioners' sugar until medium peaks form. Dollop on the tart and serve.

PREP AHEAD

The tart (without the whipped cream) can be refrigerated for up to 2 days.

LEMON CURD

MAKES **1⅔ cups**

TIME **Active 20 min;
Total 50 min**

6 **large egg yolks**

¾ **cup sugar**

1 **Tbsp. finely grated
lemon zest plus ½ cup fresh
lemon juice**

1 **stick cold unsalted butter,
cut into cubes**

This ultra-tangy, creamy lemon curd is from star chef Andrew Zimmern. It's delicious made with supermarket ingredients, but to take it up a notch, use Meyer lemons or another farmers' market citrus variety.

In a large heatproof bowl, whisk the egg yolks with the sugar, lemon zest and lemon juice. Set the bowl over a medium saucepan of simmering water and cook, stirring constantly with a wooden spoon, until thickened, 6 to 8 minutes. Remove from the heat and stir in the butter, 1 piece at a time, until incorporated. Place a sheet of plastic wrap directly onto the surface of the curd and refrigerate until chilled, about 30 minutes.

KEY LIME PIE WITH A CHOCOLATE-ALMOND CRUST

MAKES **One 10-inch pie**

TIME **Active 30 min;
Total 1 hr plus 6 hr chilling**

CRUST

6 **Tbsp. unsalted butter, melted,
plus more for greasing**

1 **cup chocolate graham cracker
crumbs (from 9 whole crackers)**

½ **cup finely ground almonds**

⅓ **cup sugar**

FILLING

1¼ **cups fresh lime juice, preferably
key lime juice (from 25 key limes)**

1 **tsp. finely grated lime zest**

**Two 14-oz. cans sweetened
condensed milk**

2 **large eggs, at room
temperature, lightly beaten**

WHIPPED CREAM

½ **cup cold heavy cream**

½ **cup cold sour cream**

2 **tsp. sugar**

**Key lime slices, for garnish
(optional)**

Elissa Bernstein, founder of the blog 17 and Baking, gives her key lime pie an unexpected twist: chocolate graham crackers and almonds in the crust. It's a terrific contrast to the creamy, tangy-sweet filling.

1 MAKE THE CRUST Preheat the oven to 375° and butter a 10-inch glass pie plate. In a food processor, pulse the graham cracker crumbs with the ground almonds and sugar until thoroughly blended. Add the melted butter and pulse until the crumbs are moistened. Press the crumbs evenly over the bottom and up the sides of the pie plate. Bake for about 20 minutes, just until the almond crumbs are lightly browned. Let the crust cool to room temperature. Leave the oven on.

2 MEANWHILE, MAKE THE FILLING In a large bowl, whisk the lime juice with the lime zest, condensed milk and eggs until smooth. Pour the filling into the cooled crust and bake for about 20 minutes, until set around the edge and slightly jiggly in the center. Let the pie cool to room temperature, then refrigerate until very firm, at least 6 hours or overnight.

3 MAKE THE WHIPPED CREAM In a bowl, using a hand mixer, beat the heavy cream and sour cream until soft peaks form, 2 minutes. Beat in the sugar until stiff peaks form, 1 minute. Mound the whipped cream on the pie. Garnish with key lime slices and serve.

PUMPKIN CHEESECAKE TART
WITH CRANBERRY GELÉE

SERVES **8 to 10**

TIME **Active 50 min; Total 4 hr 30 min**

PASTRY

- 6 Tbsp. blanched almonds
- 1½ cups plus 1 Tbsp. all-purpose flour
- 1½ sticks unsalted butter, at room temperature
- ¾ cup plus 2 Tbsp. confectioners' sugar
- 1 large egg
- ¾ tsp. pure vanilla extract
- Pinch of salt

FILLING

- 12 oz. cream cheese, at room temperature
- ½ cup packed light brown sugar
- ½ tsp. cinnamon
- ¼ tsp. ground ginger
- ⅛ tsp. ground allspice
- ⅛ tsp. ground cardamom
- ⅛ tsp. ground cloves
- Pinch of freshly ground white pepper
- Pinch of freshly grated nutmeg
- Pinch of salt
- 1¼ cups canned pumpkin puree (10 oz.)
- ¼ cup heavy cream
- 3 Tbsp. pure maple syrup
- 1½ tsp. pure vanilla extract
- 2 large eggs, at room temperature

GELÉE

- 2 cups fresh cranberries (½ lb.)
- ½ cup granulated sugar
- ¼ cup fresh orange juice
- 1½ tsp. unflavored gelatin

With its creamy filling crowned by a ruby-red cranberry gelée, this elegant pumpkin pie alternative from NYC pastry chef Deborah Racicot is a real holiday showstopper.

1 MAKE THE PASTRY In a food processor, pulse the almonds until coarsely ground. Add ½ cup of the flour and process to a fine powder; transfer to a bowl. In the food processor, pulse the butter and confectioners' sugar until creamy. Pulse in the egg and vanilla. Pulse in the remaining 1 cup plus 1 tablespoon of flour, the almond flour and the salt until a soft dough forms. Pat the pastry into a disk, wrap in plastic and refrigerate until firm, at least 1 hour.

2 Preheat the oven to 325°. On a lightly floured surface, roll out the pastry to a 14-inch round, about ⅛ inch thick. Roll the pastry onto the rolling pin and unroll it over an 11½-inch fluted tart pan with a removable bottom. Gently press the pastry into the rim. Fold in the overhanging dough and press to reinforce the sides; the sides should be twice as thick as the bottom. Trim off any excess pastry and refrigerate until firm.

3 Line the pastry with parchment paper and fill with pie weights or dried beans. Bake the pastry for about 25 minutes, until set. Remove the parchment and weights and bake for 10 minutes longer, until the crust is golden and cooked through. Let cool slightly.

4 MAKE THE FILLING In a large bowl, combine the cream cheese, brown sugar, ground spices, nutmeg and salt. Using a hand mixer, beat at medium speed until smooth. Beat in the pumpkin puree until smooth. Beat in the cream, maple syrup, vanilla and eggs at low speed until blended.

5 Put the crust on a large, sturdy baking sheet and set it in the oven. Pour the pumpkin custard into the crust. Bake for 30 to 35 minutes, until the custard is just set but still slightly jiggly in the center. Cover the edge with foil if the crust starts to brown too much. Transfer to a rack and let cool completely.

6 MAKE THE GELÉE In a medium saucepan, combine the cranberries with ½ cup of water; cook over moderate heat until they begin to pop, 5 minutes. Let cool. Puree in a blender until smooth, then strain through a fine sieve. Rinse out the saucepan. Add the sugar and ¼ cup of water to the saucepan and bring to a boil, stirring, until dissolved. Let cool. Stir in the orange juice and cranberry puree.

7 In a small bowl, sprinkle the gelatin over 2 tablespoons of water and let soften, 5 minutes. Microwave until completely melted, 10 seconds. Whisk the gelatin into the cranberry mixture and pour the gelée over the pumpkin custard; shake it gently to even it out. Refrigerate until set, at least 1 hour and up to 2 days. Remove the tart ring and serve.

PEAR-AND-CRANBERRY SLAB PIE

SERVES **8 to 10**

TIME **Active 50 min;
Total 3 hr plus cooling**

2¾ cups all-purpose flour, plus more for dusting

½ cup plus 1 Tbsp. granulated sugar

Kosher salt

2 sticks unsalted butter, cubed and chilled

½ cup ice water

4 firm Bartlett or Anjou pears—peeled, cored and cut into ¾-inch wedges

1½ cups frozen cranberries

1 tsp. ground ginger

1 large egg beaten with 1 Tbsp. water

Turbinado sugar, for sprinkling

Who says a pie has to be round? F&W's Justin Chapple forgoes the pie plate and makes this free-form, ginger-laced stunner on a rectangular baking sheet so there are slices for fruit- and crispy-edge-lovers alike.

1 In a food processor, combine 2½ cups of the flour with 1 tablespoon of the granulated sugar and 1 teaspoon of kosher salt and pulse to mix. Add the butter and pulse for 1 second at time until the mixture resembles coarse meal. Drizzle the ice water over the mixture and pulse for 1 second at a time until the dough just comes together. Turn the dough out onto a work surface, gather any crumbs and pat into 2 squares. Wrap the squares in plastic and refrigerate until chilled, about 45 minutes.

2 Preheat the oven to 400°. On a floured work surface, roll out 1 piece of the dough to a 12-inch square. Slide the dough onto a large sheet of parchment paper, then slide onto a large baking sheet. Repeat with the second piece of dough. Refrigerate for 15 minutes.

3 Slide 1 square of dough onto a work surface. In a large bowl, toss the pears with the cranberries, ginger, ½ teaspoon of salt and the remaining ½ cup of granulated sugar and ¼ cup of flour. Spread the fruit on the dough square on the baking sheet, leaving a 1-inch border. Ease the other square of dough on top of the fruit. Fold over the edge and crimp decoratively all around to seal. Brush the pie with the egg wash and sprinkle with turbinado sugar. Cut 16 small slits in the top and freeze for 15 minutes.

4 Bake the pie for about 50 minutes, until golden and the pears are tender; rotate halfway through baking. Let cool. Cut the pie into squares and serve.

MAKE AHEAD

The slab pie can be stored at room temperature for up to 2 days.

SERVE WITH

Vanilla ice cream.

BROWN BUTTER PECAN PIE
WITH ESPRESSO DATES

MAKES   **One 9-inch pie**

TIME   **Active 1 hr; Total 5 hr 15 min plus cooling**

CRUST

1¼ cups all-purpose flour, plus more for dusting

1½ tsp. granulated sugar

½ tsp. kosher salt

1 stick unsalted butter, cubed and frozen

Ice water

FILLING

2 cups pecan halves (7 oz.)

½ lb. Medjool dates, pitted and chopped (1 cup)

3 Tbsp. brewed espresso or strong coffee

1 stick unsalted butter

1 cup packed light brown sugar

1 cup Lyle's Golden Syrup or light corn syrup

1½ tsp. instant espresso powder

1½ tsp. kosher salt

3 large eggs

Whipped cream, for serving

This filling is swirled with toasty brown butter and studded with rich and chewy dates cooked in espresso, which helps cut the sweetness you expect in most pecan pies. The recipe was adapted from the *Soframiz* cookbook by Maura Kilpatrick and Ana Sortun of Sofra bakery in Boston.

1 MAKE THE CRUST In a food processor, pulse the 1¼ cups of flour with the granulated sugar and salt. Add the butter and pulse until it is the size of small peas. Add ¼ cup of ice water and pulse until the dough is evenly moistened. Gradually add more water if needed. Turn out the dough onto a work surface and knead 2 or 3 times, just until it comes together. Form the dough into a disk, wrap in plastic and refrigerate until firm, about 1 hour.

2 On a lightly floured work surface, roll out the dough to a 12-inch round; transfer to a 9-inch pie plate. Fold the edge of the dough under itself and crimp. Freeze the crust for at least 2 hours or overnight.

3 Preheat the oven to 375°. Line the crust with parchment paper and fill with pie weights or dried beans. Bake for about 25 minutes, until lightly browned around the edge. Remove the paper and weights and bake until the bottom is lightly browned, about 10 minutes longer. Let the crust cool completely.

4 MEANWHILE, MAKE THE FILLING Reduce the oven temperature to 350°. Spread the pecans on a rimmed baking sheet and toast until fragrant, 8 to 10 minutes. Let cool completely.

5 In a small skillet, cook the dates in the brewed espresso over moderate heat, stirring, until very soft, 3 to 5 minutes. Scrape the mixture into a small bowl and wipe out the skillet.

6 Add the butter to the skillet and cook over moderate heat, swirling, until the milk solids turn a deep golden brown, about 5 minutes. Let cool slightly.

7 In a large bowl, whisk the brown sugar with the golden syrup, espresso powder and salt. Whisk in the eggs, then gradually whisk in the brown butter until the filling is smooth.

8 Set the pie plate on a rimmed baking sheet. Spread the espresso dates in the crust and scatter the pecans on top. Pour the filling over the pecans. Bake for about 1 hour and 15 minutes, until the filling is set around the edge and slightly jiggly in the center. Transfer the pie to a rack and let cool completely. Serve with whipped cream.

MAKE AHEAD

The pie can be covered and kept at room temperature for 3 days. The unbaked crust can be wrapped in plastic and frozen for 1 month.

TEXAS STATE FAIR PECAN PIE

MAKES   **One 10-inch pie**

TIME   **Active 40 min;
Total 3 hr 30 min plus
cooling**

PIE SHELL

- 2 **cups all-purpose flour, plus
  more for dusting**
- 1 **Tbsp. granulated sugar**
- 1 **tsp. salt**
- 1 **stick plus 4 Tbsp. unsalted
  butter, cut into ½-inch dice**
- ¼ **cup plus 1 Tbsp. ice water**

FILLING

- 1½ **cups pecan halves (5½ oz.)**
- 1½ **sticks cold unsalted butter**
- 1½ **cups dark brown sugar**
- ¾ **cup granulated sugar**
- ½ **cup light corn syrup**
- 3 **Tbsp. whole milk**
- 2 **Tbsp. all-purpose flour**
- ½ **vanilla bean, split and seeds
  scraped**
- ½ **tsp. salt**
- 4 **large eggs**
  **Unsweetened whipped cream or
  vanilla ice cream, for serving**

This extraordinarily rich and sweet pecan pie was the winner at the 1996 State Fair of Texas pie competition, which Dallas chef Dean Fearing helped judge. "Out of 140 pies, this one was it," he says. "The baker's name was Bobby Lee; she never told me her last name." It's become a Fearing family go-to since then.

1 MAKE THE PIE SHELL In a food processor, pulse the 2 cups of flour with the sugar and salt. Add the butter and pulse until it is the size of small peas. Add the ice water and pulse until the pastry is evenly moistened. Turn it out onto a work surface and knead 2 or 3 times, just until it comes together. Form into a disk, wrap in plastic and refrigerate until firm, about 1 hour.

2 Preheat the oven to 350°. On a lightly floured surface, roll out the pastry ⅛ inch thick; transfer to a deep 10-inch glass pie plate and trim the overhang to ½ inch. Fold the edge of the pastry under itself and crimp. Prick the bottom with a fork in a few places. Freeze for 30 minutes.

3 Line the pie shell with parchment paper and fill with pie weights or dried beans. Bake for about 25 minutes, until lightly browned around the edge. Remove the paper and weights and bake the shell for 15 minutes longer, until lightly golden. Leave the oven on.

4 MAKE THE FILLING In a pie plate, toast the pecans for about 8 minutes, until lightly browned. Let cool.

5 In a medium saucepan, melt the butter. Add the brown sugar, granulated sugar, corn syrup, milk, flour, vanilla seeds and salt. Cook over moderate heat just until the mixture comes to a boil. Remove from the heat and let stand for 5 minutes.

6 In a heatproof bowl, lightly beat the eggs. Gradually whisk in the hot sugar mixture until thoroughly blended. Spread the toasted pecans in the pie shell and pour the filling on top. Bake for about 45 minutes, until the center is just barely set and the crust is golden brown. Transfer the pie to a rack to cool completely. Serve with unsweetened whipped cream or vanilla ice cream.

MAKE AHEAD

The pie can be covered and kept at room temperature for 1 day. The pie shell can be wrapped well and frozen for up to 1 month.

> "Holidays aren't the time to mess with classics. This recipe, though, wisely calls for prebaking the dough, so the crust isn't soggy and underbaked—a common problem and a pet peeve of mine in pumpkin pies."
> —KATE HEDDINGS, EXECUTIVE FOOD EDITOR

CLASSIC PUMPKIN PIE

MAKES **One 9-inch pie**

TIME **Active 30 min; Total 2 hr 30 min plus cooling**

DOUGH

- 1¼ cups all-purpose flour, plus more for dusting
- Pinch of salt
- 1 stick cold unsalted butter, cubed
- ¼ cup ice water

FILLING

- 4 large eggs
- ¾ cup sugar
- 1 Tbsp. cornstarch
- 2 tsp. cinnamon
- ¼ tsp. ground cloves
- Pinch of salt
- One 15-oz. can pumpkin puree
- ½ cup heavy cream

To create a crisp crust on the bottom, cookbook author Grace Parisi partially bakes the pie shell before adding the filling. If the edge starts to darken too much, cover it with a pie shield or strips of foil.

1 MAKE THE DOUGH In a food processor, pulse the 1¼ cups of flour with the salt. Add the butter and pulse until it is the size of peas. Drizzle in the water and pulse until the crumbs are moistened; turn out onto a work surface. Gather the dough into a ball, flatten, wrap in plastic and refrigerate for 30 minutes.

2 Preheat the oven to 350°. On a lightly floured surface, roll out the dough to a 13-inch round, a scant ¼ inch thick. Fit the dough into a 9-inch glass pie plate and trim the overhang to ¾ inch. Fold the dough under itself and crimp decoratively; refrigerate the pie shell for 10 minutes.

3 Line the pie shell with foil and fill with pie weights or dried beans. Bake in the center of the oven until nearly set, about 25 minutes. Remove the foil and weights and bake until the crust is pale golden, about 10 minutes. Let cool slightly.

4 MAKE THE FILLING In a medium bowl, whisk the eggs with the sugar, cornstarch, cinnamon, cloves and salt until smooth. Whisk in the pumpkin puree, then the cream. Working near the oven, pour the filling into the crust. Bake for about 45 minutes, until the custard is set. Let the pie cool on a rack.

SALTED CARAMEL PIE

SERVES **8 to 10**

TIME **Active 30 min; Total 2 hr 30 min plus 4 hr chilling**

1¼ cups graham cracker crumbs (about 5 oz.)

4 Tbsp. unsalted butter, melted

¼ cup light brown sugar

Two 14-oz. cans sweetened condensed milk

Fleur de sel

Nonstick cooking spray

2 cups heavy cream

2 Tbsp. confectioners' sugar

This super-easy caramel lover's dream pie is from L.A. chef Carrie Cusack. The filling is made with sweetened condensed milk sprinkled lightly with sea salt and baked until thick and gooey. It's then spooned into a simple graham cracker crust and chilled.

1 Preheat the oven to 350°. In a food processor, pulse the graham cracker crumbs with the melted butter and light brown sugar until the crumbs are moistened. Press the crumbs evenly into a 9-inch glass or metal pie plate. Bake the crust for about 10 minutes, just until lightly browned. Let cool. Increase the oven temperature to 425°.

2 Scrape the condensed milk into a 9-by-13-inch glass baking dish and sprinkle with a scant ½ teaspoon of fleur de sel. Cover the dish with foil and place it in a roasting pan. Add enough hot water to the pan to reach one-third of the way up the side of the baking dish. Bake, lifting the foil to stir the condensed milk 2 or 3 times, until it's golden and thickened, about 2 hours; add more water to the roasting pan as necessary. The consistency of the caramel should be like dulce de leche. Don't worry if it is lumpy; it will smooth out as it chills.

3 Scrape the caramel filling into the pie crust, smoothing the top. Spray a sheet of plastic wrap with nonstick spray and cover the pie. Refrigerate until the filling is chilled and set, at least 4 hours.

4 In a bowl, using a hand mixer, beat the cream with the confectioners' sugar until firm. Remove the plastic from the pie. Mound the whipped cream on top and sprinkle with fleur de sel. Cut into wedges and serve.

PREP AHEAD

The recipe can be prepared through Step 2 up to 5 days ahead. Refrigerate the crust and filling separately.

GOLDEN CARAMEL AND CHOCOLATE TART

MAKES	One 9-inch tart
TIME	Active 40 min; Total 3 hr 30 min plus 2 hr chilling

PASTRY

- 1½ cups all-purpose flour
- ½ cup confectioners' sugar
- ¼ tsp. kosher salt
- 1 stick plus 1 Tbsp. cold unsalted butter, cut into ½-inch dice
- 1 large egg yolk

FILLING

- 2 oz. bittersweet chocolate, chopped
- ⅔ cup granulated sugar
- ¼ tsp. fresh lemon juice
- 4 Tbsp. unsalted butter, cut into 4 pieces
- 1¼ cups heavy cream, at room temperature
- ½ tsp. kosher salt
- 4 large egg yolks

Cookbook author Dorie Greenspan has perfected all the elements of this phenomenal tart, from the buttery pastry to the rich filling. "This caramel is easy to get right," she says. "It just shouldn't color too much. When the sugar turns the color of pale ale, it's ready."

1 MAKE THE PASTRY In a food processor, pulse the flour with the confectioners' sugar and salt. Add the butter and pulse until it's the size of peas. Add the egg yolk and pulse for 10 seconds at a time until incorporated, about 4 long pulses. Transfer the pastry to a sheet of parchment paper, shape into a disk and cover with another sheet of parchment paper. Roll out the pastry to a 12-inch round. Slide the pastry on the parchment paper onto a baking sheet and refrigerate until firm, about 1 hour.

2 Let the pastry stand at room temperature for 5 minutes to soften. Discard the top sheet of parchment and invert the pastry into a 9-inch fluted tart pan with a removable bottom; fit the pastry into the pan and trim the overhang. Prick the pastry all over with a fork and refrigerate for 30 minutes.

3 Preheat the oven to 400°. Line the tart shell with parchment paper and fill with pie weights or dried beans. Bake until the pastry is set and lightly browned at the edge, about 20 minutes. Remove the parchment and weights and bake the pastry for 5 minutes more, until lightly browned on the bottom. Transfer to a rack to cool completely. Reduce the oven temperature to 325°.

4 MAKE THE FILLING In a microwave-safe small bowl, microwave the chocolate at high power for 30 seconds at a time just until melted. Let cool slightly.

5 Pour the chocolate into the tart shell, spreading it evenly over the bottom. In a small skillet, stir ⅓ cup of the granulated sugar with the lemon juice and ¼ cup of water over moderately high heat until the sugar dissolves. Cook, without stirring, until the mixture starts to color, about 5 minutes. Continue cooking, stirring constantly with a heatproof spatula, until a lightly golden caramel forms, about 5 minutes. Remove the skillet from the heat; stir in the butter, 1 piece at a time. Stir in the cream and salt; let the caramel cool to room temperature.

6 In a medium bowl, whisk the egg yolks with the remaining ⅓ cup of granulated sugar until smooth. Stir the caramel into the egg yolk mixture, then pour the custard over the chocolate in the tart shell. Transfer the tart to a foil-lined baking sheet. Bake until the crust is browned and the filling is still slightly wobbly in the middle, 30 minutes. Transfer the tart to a rack and let cool to room temperature. Refrigerate until set and thoroughly chilled, at least 2 hours. Unmold and serve chilled or at room temperature.

CHOCOLATE CREAM PIE

MAKES **One 9-inch pie**

TIME **40 min plus 3 hr chilling**

CRUST

- 6 oz. chocolate wafer cookies, finely ground
- 4½ Tbsp. unsalted butter, melted
- 2 Tbsp. sugar
  Pinch of fine sea salt

FILLING

- 2 cups whole milk
- ½ cup plus 2 Tbsp. sugar
- 3 egg yolks
- ¼ cup cornstarch
- ¼ tsp. fine sea salt
- 4 oz. semisweet chocolate, chopped
- 1 oz. unsweetened chocolate, chopped
- ¾ cup heavy cream
- 1 tsp. pure vanilla extract
  Chocolate shavings, for garnish

Recipe developer Melissa Rubel Jacobson turns pudding into a homey, silky pie by adding a quick chocolate crust and whipped cream. "But you could still serve just the filling as a pudding," she says.

1 MAKE THE CRUST Preheat the oven to 350°. In a medium bowl, mix the cookie crumbs with the butter, sugar and salt until the crumbs are evenly moistened. Scrape the crumbs into a 9-inch glass pie dish and press them evenly over the bottom and up the sides. Bake the crust for about 8 minutes, until fragrant. Remove from the oven and, using the bottom of a drinking glass, immediately press the crumbs to compact the crust. Let cool completely.

2 MAKE THE FILLING In a medium saucepan, heat the milk with ¼ cup of the sugar until bubbles form around the edge. In a large bowl, whisk the egg yolks with ¼ cup of the sugar, the cornstarch and salt. Gradually whisk in the hot milk. Pour this mixture into the saucepan and cook over moderate heat, whisking constantly, until very thick, about 3 minutes. Remove from the heat and whisk in the semisweet and unsweetened chocolates until smooth. Strain the filling through a coarse sieve into the pie crust and smooth the surface with a rubber spatula. Press a piece of plastic wrap directly onto the surface of the filling and refrigerate until chilled, at least 3 hours.

3 Let the pie stand at room temperature for 10 minutes. Meanwhile, in a medium bowl, beat the heavy cream with the remaining 2 tablespoons of sugar and the vanilla until firm. Spread the whipped cream over the pie, cut into wedges and serve, garnished with chocolate shavings.

MAKE AHEAD

The pie can be refrigerated for up to 1 day.

MILK CHOCOLATE BANANA PIE

MAKES   One 9-inch pie

TIME   Active 30 min;
       Total 2 hr plus 4 hr chilling

CRUST

¼ cup hazelnuts

1 stick unsalted butter, softened, plus more for greasing

⅓ cup sugar

1 large egg yolk

½ tsp. pure vanilla extract

1 cup plus 3 Tbsp. all-purpose flour

Pinch of salt

FILLING

1 cup heavy cream

3 large egg yolks

¾ lb. milk chocolate, chopped

2 Tbsp. unsalted butter

1 tsp. pure vanilla extract

2 large bananas, sliced ¼ inch thick

1 Tbsp. sugar

1 Tbsp. dark rum

Will Packwood, a chef-instructor at the Auguste Escoffier School of Culinary Arts in Austin, creates a grown-up take on a childhood favorite: Nutella with bananas. He layers rum-spiked bananas with a luscious chocolate cream, all in a buttery hazelnut crust.

1 MAKE THE CRUST Preheat the oven to 350°. Spread the hazelnuts in a pie plate and toast for about 12 minutes, until fragrant and blistered. Rub the nuts in a kitchen towel to remove the skins. Finely grind the nuts in a food processor, then transfer to a small bowl.

2 Wipe out the processor. Add the stick of butter and the sugar and process until fluffy. Add the egg yolk and vanilla and process until just blended. Add the flour, salt and the ground hazelnuts and pulse until a crumbly dough forms.

3 Scrape the dough into a large disk, then press it into a 9-inch fluted tart pan with a removable bottom. Line the dough with plastic wrap and press evenly into the pan. Freeze until firm, 10 minutes.

4 Discard the plastic and press a piece of well-buttered foil directly onto the dough. Fill the foil with pie weights or dried beans and bake for about 30 minutes, until the shell is golden around the edge. Remove the foil and weights and bake for 15 minutes longer, until golden all over. Let cool on a rack.

5 MAKE THE FILLING In a medium saucepan, bring the cream to a boil. Remove from the heat. In a medium bowl, whisk half of the warm cream with the egg yolks. Return the cream to the saucepan and whisk constantly over moderately low heat until an instant-read thermometer registers 160°. Remove from the heat and immediately stir in the chocolate, butter and vanilla and whisk until smooth. Let the filling cool to room temperature.

6 In a medium bowl, toss the bananas with the sugar and rum. Arrange the bananas in a single overlapping layer in the tart shell and spoon the chocolate cream on top. Smooth the surface with a warmed offset spatula. Refrigerate the tart until firm, at least 4 hours, before serving.

MILK CHOCOLATE TART
WITH A PRETZEL CRUST

SERVES **8**

TIME **Active 45 min;
Total 2 hr 45 min plus 4 hr
chilling**

CRUST

1 **stick unsalted butter, softened**

1¼ **cups coarsely crushed thin
pretzels (3½ oz.)**

¾ **cup confectioners' sugar**

½ **cup all-purpose flour**

1 **large egg**

2 **oz. bittersweet chocolate,
melted**

FILLING

1½ **cups heavy cream**

¾ **lb. milk chocolate, chopped**

**Maldon sea salt, crushed
pretzels and crème fraîche,
for serving**

This salty-sweet dessert from
New York City pastry chef
Colleen Grapes is a tribute to
the chocolate-covered pretzel.
Make a crunchy crust with
crushed pretzels, pour in a
luxurious milk chocolate filling,
then sprinkle more crushed
pretzels on top.

1 MAKE THE CRUST In a stand
mixer fitted with the paddle, beat
the butter with ¾ cup of the
pretzels and the confectioners'
sugar at low speed until creamy.
Beat in the flour and egg. Add the
remaining ½ cup of pretzels,
being sure to leave some pretzel
pieces intact. Flatten the dough
between 2 sheets of plastic wrap
and refrigerate until chilled, at
least 30 minutes.

2 Preheat the oven to 350°. Roll
out the dough between the sheets
of plastic wrap to a 12-inch round.
Peel off the top sheet and invert
the dough over a 10-inch fluted
tart pan with a removable bottom.
Press the dough into the corners
and patch any tears. Trim the
overhanging dough and refrigerate
the shell for 30 minutes, until firm.

3 Line the shell with parchment
paper and fill with pie weights. Bake
for about 30 minutes, until
nearly set. Remove the parchment
and weights and bake for 10 to
15 minutes longer, until the tart
shell is firm; cover the edge with
foil if it darkens too much. Let the
shell cool completely. Brush the
melted chocolate over the bottom
and up the sides and refrigerate
for 10 minutes, until set.

4 MEANWHILE, MAKE THE FILLING
In a medium saucepan, bring the
cream to a simmer. Off the heat,
add the milk chocolate and let
stand for 5 minutes, then whisk
until smooth. Transfer the
filling to a bowl and let cool to room
temperature, about 1 hour.

5 Pour the filling into the shell
and refrigerate until set, at least
4 hours. Sprinkle lightly with
sea salt and crushed pretzels. Cut
the tart into wedges, top with
crème fraîche and serve.

COCONUT CREAM PIE

MAKES   One 9-inch pie

TIME   Active 1 hr 10 min;
Total 4 hr 10 min

FILLING

1½ cups unsweetened coconut milk

1 tsp. unflavored powdered
gelatin

2 cups heavy cream

⅓ cup granulated sugar

1½ Tbsp. corn syrup

½ tsp. kosher salt

1 vanilla bean, split and seeds
scraped

2½ Tbsp. cornstarch mixed with
2 Tbsp. water

2 Tbsp. unsalted butter

¼ cup plus 2 Tbsp. sweetened
cream of coconut,
such as Coco Lopez

CRUST

3 cups Nilla Wafer cookies,
crushed (1 cup packed)

½ cup sweetened shredded
coconut

1 Tbsp. all-purpose flour

1 Tbsp. granulated sugar

1 Tbsp. turbinado sugar

½ tsp. kosher salt

5 Tbsp. unsalted butter, melted

Toasted coconut flakes,
for garnish

New York City pastry chef Kierin Baldwin has a thing for pies. For this recipe, she takes the coconut flavor to the max, adding it to each component of the pie: the crust, the filling and the topping.

1 MAKE THE FILLING In a small bowl, whisk ¼ cup of the coconut milk with the gelatin. In a medium saucepan, combine the remaining 1¼ cups of coconut milk with ½ cup of the heavy cream. Add the granulated sugar, corn syrup, ¼ teaspoon of the salt and the vanilla bean and seeds; bring just to a simmer over moderately high heat. Whisk in the cornstarch mixture and bring to a boil, then simmer, whisking constantly, until thickened, about 3 minutes. Remove the pan from the heat and whisk in the gelatin mixture until dissolved, then whisk in the butter and ¼ cup of the cream of coconut. Strain the filling through a fine sieve into a heatproof bowl; discard the vanilla bean. Press a sheet of plastic wrap directly on the surface of the filling and let cool, then refrigerate until well chilled, about 1 hour.

2 MEANWHILE, MAKE THE CRUST Preheat the oven to 325°. In a food processor, pulse the cookies with all of the remaining ingredients except the toasted coconut. Transfer the crumbs to a 9-inch metal pie plate. Press the crumbs evenly over the bottom and up the sides of the pie plate, forming a ¼-inch edge over the rim of the plate. Bake the crust for 10 to 12 minutes, rotating halfway through baking, until dry and lightly browned. Let cool.

3 In a large bowl, using a hand mixer, beat the remaining 1½ cups of heavy cream, 2 tablespoons of cream of coconut and ¼ teaspoon of salt until firm. Fold one-third of the whipped cream into the chilled filling until no streaks remain. Spread the filling in the crust. Mound the remaining whipped cream on top and refrigerate the pie for at least 2 hours. Garnish with toasted coconut before serving.

MAKE AHEAD

The coconut cream pie can be refrigerated overnight.

TORTA DELLA NONNA

SERVES **8**

TIME **Active 30 min; Total 2 hr**

PASTRY

- 3 cups all-purpose flour, plus more for dusting
- ½ cup sugar
- 1 tsp. baking powder
  Finely grated zest of 1 lemon
- ¼ tsp. salt
- 1 stick plus 6 Tbsp. unsalted butter, softened, plus more for greasing
- 2 large eggs plus 4 large egg yolks

PASTRY CREAM

- 2 cups milk
- ½ cup sugar
- ½ vanilla bean, split and seeds scraped
  Two 2-by-1-inch strips of lemon zest
- 5 large egg yolks
- ⅓ cup all-purpose flour
  Toasted pine nuts and fresh berries, for serving

"Grandmother's cake" is a traditional Tuscan dish, though everyone's nonna makes the simple creamy dessert slightly differently. In his rendition, Joe Sponzo, a longtime private chef to Sting and Trudie Styler, fills a delicate pastry crust with vanilla-and-lemon-scented pastry cream (other Tuscan cooks add ricotta cheese). He tops the tart with pine nuts, another regional staple.

1 MAKE THE PASTRY In a food processor, combine the 3 cups of flour with the sugar, baking powder, lemon zest and salt. Add the softened butter in clumps and pulse until the mixture resembles coarse meal. Add the whole eggs and egg yolks and pulse a few times, until the dough just comes together. Turn the dough out onto a lightly floured work surface and knead 2 or 3 times, just until it comes together. Divide the dough into 2 pieces, 1 slightly smaller than the other. Pat into disks, wrap each in plastic and refrigerate for at least 30 minutes.

2 MAKE THE PASTRY CREAM In a medium saucepan, heat the milk with ¼ cup of the sugar, the vanilla bean and seeds and the lemon zest until hot to the touch. In a medium bowl, whisk the egg yolks with the remaining ¼ cup of sugar until blended. Stir in the flour until incorporated, then whisk in the hot milk in a thin stream.

3 Set a fine-mesh strainer over another medium bowl. Pour the pastry cream mixture back into the saucepan and cook over moderate heat, whisking, until thick and bubbling, about 2 minutes. Immediately strain the pastry cream into the bowl, scraping the strainer with a rubber spatula. Press a sheet of plastic wrap directly onto the surface of the pastry cream and refrigerate until chilled, 1 to 2 hours.

4 Preheat the oven to 350°. Butter and flour a 10-inch fluted tart pan with a removable bottom. On a lightly floured work surface, roll out the larger disk of pastry to an ⅛-inch-thick round. Ease the pastry into the tart pan, pressing the dough into the corners. Don't trim the overhang.

5 Spread the chilled pastry cream in the tart shell in an even layer. Roll out the remaining pastry disk to an ⅛-inch-thick round and set it over the tart; gently press out any air bubbles. Carefully roll the rolling pin over the tart pan rim to cut off the overhanging dough. Gently press the edges together to seal the tart.

6 Bake the tart in the lower third of the oven for about 40 minutes, rotating the pan halfway through, until the crust is golden brown. Let the tart cool completely in the pan, then unmold and transfer to a serving plate. Sprinkle with pine nuts, cut into wedges and serve with berries.

LEMON ICEBOX PIE

MAKES One 9-inch pie

TIME Active 30 min; Total 1 hr plus 7 hr cooling and freezing

14 whole graham crackers, broken

¼ cup sugar

¼ tsp. salt

6 Tbsp. unsalted butter, melted

Two 14-oz. cans sweetened condensed milk

1¼ cups fresh lemon juice plus 2 Tbsp. finely grated lemon zest

8 large egg yolks

This silken, no-bake frozen pie is from David Guas of Bayou Bakery in Washington, DC. He adapted the recipe from the signature dessert at Clancy's, one of his favorite neighborhood restaurants in his native New Orleans.

1 Preheat the oven to 325°. In a food processor, pulse the graham crackers with the sugar and salt until finely ground but not powdery. Add the butter and pulse until the crumbs are evenly moistened; transfer to a 9-inch springform pan and press into the bottom and two-thirds of the way up the sides. Set the pan on a rimmed baking sheet.

2 In a medium bowl, whisk the condensed milk with the lemon juice. In another bowl, using a hand mixer, beat the lemon zest with the egg yolks until pale.

Beat in the condensed milk mixture until smooth. Pour the filling into the crust.

3 Bake the pie for 25 minutes, until the center jiggles slightly and the edge is set. Transfer the pan to a rack; let cool for 1 hour. Loosely cover the pan with plastic wrap and freeze the pie for at least 6 hours or overnight.

4 Wrap a warm, damp kitchen towel around the sides of the springform pan to release the pie; remove the ring. Using a hot knife, slice the pie and serve.

SERVE WITH

Whipped cream.

"This pie is a little dose of sunshine in the cool months, when lemons are at their peak. Or maybe that's the vitamin C boost talking. It has more condensed milk and less lemon juice than some versions, so it's creamier and a bit sweeter but still has that great lemony tang." —CHRISTINE QUINLAN, DEPUTY EDITOR

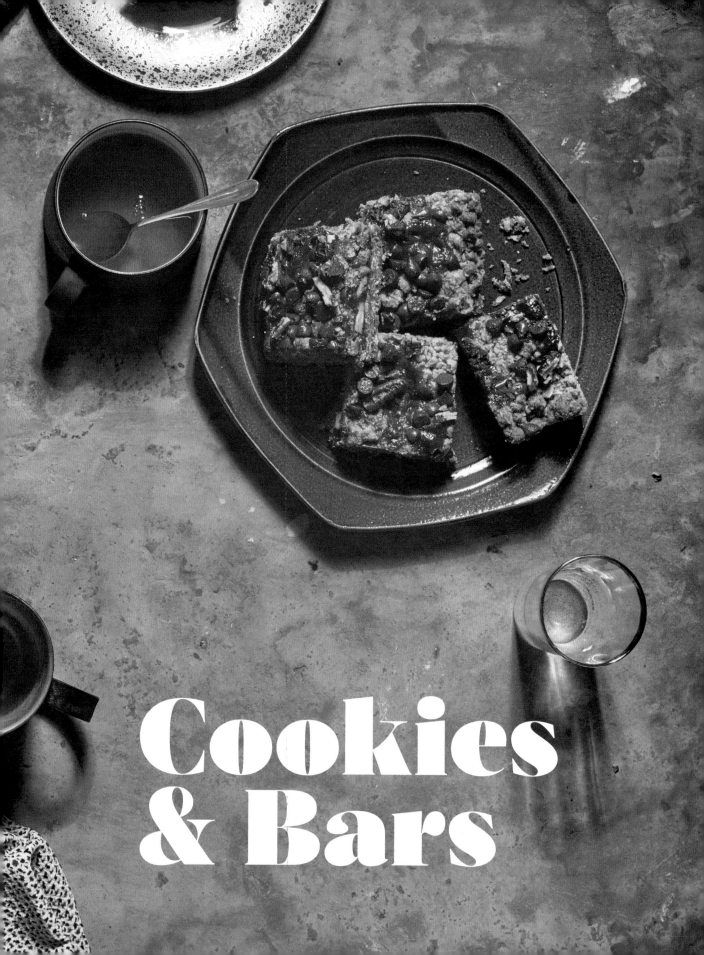

Cookies & Bars

CHOCOLATE CHUNK COOKIE FOR ONE

MAKES 1

TIME Active 5 min; Total 25 min

- 1 Tbsp. unsalted butter
- 1 Tbsp. packed light brown sugar
- 1 tsp. granulated sugar
- ⅛ tsp. pure vanilla extract
- Maldon salt
- 2 Tbsp. all-purpose flour
- 1½ Tbsp. dark chocolate chunks

Cookies always hit the spot, but you don't have to bake an entire batch to get your sweet fix. Just make this single chewy-crisp one from F&W's Justin Chapple in the toaster oven. Note: The photo, opposite, is not to scale!

Preheat a toaster oven to 350°. In a small microwave-safe bowl, heat the butter until just softened, about 10 seconds. Using a fork, blend in both sugars, the vanilla and a pinch of salt. Blend in the flour, then stir in the chocolate chunks. Scoop the batter onto a parchment paper–lined toaster tray; sprinkle with salt. Bake until lightly browned, 13 to 15 minutes. Let cool slightly before eating.

COCOA NIB–CHOCOLATE CHIP COOKIES

MAKES About 6½ dozen

TIME Active 30 min; Total 1 hr 15 min plus cooling

- 2½ cups all-purpose flour
- ½ tsp. baking soda
- ½ tsp. salt
- 2 sticks unsalted butter, softened
- 1¼ cups sugar
- 1 large egg yolk
- 1 tsp. pure vanilla extract
- Two 3-oz. milk chocolate bars with cocoa nibs, finely chopped

Those who prefer crispy over soft cookies will love this recipe. For an ingenious twist on the classic, cookbook author Grace Parisi uses chocolate with cocoa nibs instead of the usual chips.

1 In a medium bowl, whisk the flour, baking soda and salt. In a stand mixer fitted with the paddle, or using a hand mixer in a large bowl, beat the butter with the sugar at medium speed until light and fluffy, 3 minutes. Beat in the egg yolk and vanilla, scraping the sides and bottom of the bowl. Beat in the dry ingredients at medium-low speed, then fold in the chocolate. Divide the dough in half. Pat each half into a round, wrap in plastic and refrigerate for 15 minutes.

2 Preheat the oven to 350° and position racks in the upper and lower thirds. On a lightly floured surface, roll out each piece of dough ⅛ inch thick. Using a 2-inch biscuit cutter, stamp out rounds as close together as possible. Arrange the rounds on large baking sheets, about 1 inch apart. Gather the scraps and reroll, cutting out more cookies.

3 Bake the cookies in batches until golden, about 20 minutes; shift the pans from top to bottom and front to back halfway through. Let the cookies cool on the sheets for 5 minutes, then transfer to racks to cool completely.

PREP AHEAD

The cookie dough can be wrapped in plastic and foil and frozen for up to 1 month. Thaw in the refrigerator before using.

MILK CHOCOLATE COOKIES
WITH MALTED CREAM

MAKES	About 30 sandwich cookies
TIME	Active 30 min; Total 1 hr 30 min

COOKIES

1½ sticks unsalted butter, softened

½ cup light brown sugar

½ cup granulated sugar

6 oz. milk chocolate, melted and cooled slightly

1 Tbsp. pure vanilla extract

1¾ cups all-purpose flour

2 Tbsp. unsweetened cocoa powder

1 tsp. baking soda

½ tsp. salt

FILLING

1 stick unsalted butter, softened

½ cup chocolate malt powder, such as Ovaltine

½ tsp. pure vanilla extract

2 cups confectioners' sugar

Mathew Rice, pastry chef at Pastaria in Nashville, grew up loving an Oreo-like cookie called Murray Chocolate Cremes. In this homage, he creates a perfectly malty filling for milk chocolate wafers by mixing butter and sugar with Ovaltine.

1 MAKE THE COOKIES Preheat the oven to 350° and position racks in the lower and middle thirds. Line 2 baking sheets with parchment.

2 In a large bowl, using a hand mixer, beat the butter with the brown sugar and granulated sugar at medium speed until smooth. Add the chocolate and vanilla and beat until smooth. In a small bowl, whisk the flour with the cocoa powder, baking soda and salt. Add the dry ingredients to the butter mixture and beat at low speed just until incorporated. Roll the dough between 2 sheets of parchment paper to a scant ¼-inch thickness and refrigerate until firm, about 15 minutes.

3 Using a 2-inch round cookie cutter, stamp out as many rounds as possible and transfer to the prepared baking sheets, 1 inch apart. Gather the scraps and chill, with the cut-out rounds, for 10 minutes. Reroll the scraps and stamp out more rounds.

4 Bake the cookies for about 10 minutes, until dry and set; shift the pans halfway through baking. Transfer the cookies to a rack and let cool completely.

5 MAKE THE FILLING In a medium bowl, using a hand mixer, beat the butter with the chocolate malt powder at medium speed until light, about 3 minutes. Add the vanilla and confectioners' sugar and beat at low speed just until combined. Transfer the filling to a pastry bag fitted with a ½-inch plain tip. Arrange half of the cookies on a work surface, bottom side up, and pipe a 1-inch mound of filling onto each one. Sandwich with the remaining cookies, pressing to spread the filling to the edges, and serve.

> "These cookies are so beloved by *Food & Wine* editors, we have them at practically every staff party. They're intensely chocolaty—just one makes me delirious. So, of course, I usually have three at a time."
>
> —SUSAN CHOUNG, BOOKS EDITOR

CHOCOLATE BROWNIE COOKIES

MAKES   **About 3 dozen**

TIME   **Active 30 min;
Total 2 hr 30 min
plus cooling**

- **1 lb. semisweet chocolate, chopped**
- **4 Tbsp. unsalted butter**
- **4 large eggs, at room temperature**
- **1½ cups sugar**
- **1 tsp. pure vanilla extract**
- **¼ tsp. salt**
- **½ cup all-purpose flour, sifted**
- **½ tsp. baking powder**
- **One 12-oz. bag semisweet chocolate chips**

These double-chocolate cookies are like crispy-chewy brownies in cookie form. Belinda Leong of B. Patisserie in San Francisco freezes the batter before baking in order to achieve that crackly outer layer.

1 In a large bowl set over a saucepan of simmering water, melt the chopped chocolate with the butter, stirring a few times, until smooth, about 7 minutes.

2 In another large bowl, using a hand mixer, beat the eggs with the sugar at medium speed until thick and pale, about 5 minutes. Beat in the vanilla and salt. Using a rubber spatula, fold in the melted chocolate, then fold in the flour and baking powder. Stir in the chocolate chips. Scrape the batter into a shallow baking dish, cover and freeze until well chilled and firm, about 1 hour.

3 Preheat the oven to 350° and line 2 baking sheets with parchment paper. Working in batches, scoop 2-tablespoon-size mounds of dough onto the prepared baking sheets, about 2 inches apart. Bake until the cookies are dry around the edges and cracked on top, 10 minutes. Let the cookies cool on the baking sheets for 10 minutes, then transfer to a rack to cool completely before serving.

MAKE AHEAD

The cookies can be stored in an airtight container for up to 4 days.

FUDGY CHOCOLATE–WALNUT COOKIES

MAKES 1 dozen

TIME Active 25 min;
Total 45 min plus cooling

2¾ cups walnut halves (9 oz.)

3 cups confectioners' sugar

½ cup plus 3 Tbsp. unsweetened Dutch-process cocoa powder

¼ tsp. salt

4 large egg whites, at room temperature

1 Tbsp. pure vanilla extract

New York City pastry chef François Payard's divinely gooey chocolate-walnut cookies are flourless, which makes them ideal for gluten-free-dessert lovers.

1 Preheat the oven to 350° and position racks in the upper and lower thirds. Line 2 large rimmed baking sheets with parchment paper.

2 Spread the walnut halves on another large rimmed baking sheet and toast in the oven for about 9 minutes, until golden and fragrant. Let cool slightly, then finely chop them.

3 In a large bowl, whisk the confectioners' sugar with the cocoa powder and salt. Whisk in the chopped walnuts. Add the egg whites and vanilla and beat just until the batter is moistened (be careful not to overbeat or it will stiffen). Spoon the batter onto the prepared baking sheets in 12 evenly spaced mounds.

4 Bake the cookies for about 20 minutes, until the tops are glossy, lightly cracked and firm to the touch; shift the pans from front to back and top to bottom halfway through.

5 Slide the parchment paper (with the cookies) onto 2 wire racks to cool completely before serving.

MAKE AHEAD

The cookies can be stored in an airtight container for up to 3 days.

"I love a great flourless chocolate cookie, and François Payard's version is as good as it gets. Super-chocolaty and nutty, it hits the ideal cookie trifecta: chewy, crisp and fudgy."
—JUSTIN CHAPPLE, TEST KITCHEN DEPUTY EDITOR

OATMEAL-CHERRY COOKIES

MAKES 18

TIME Active 30 min;
Total 1 hr plus cooling

¾ cup all-purpose flour
½ cup whole-wheat flour
½ tsp. baking soda
½ tsp. kosher salt
½ tsp. cinnamon
¼ tsp. freshly grated nutmeg
2 sticks unsalted butter, softened
1 cup granulated sugar
½ cup packed light brown sugar
2 large eggs
2 tsp. pure vanilla extract
2 cups old-fashioned rolled oats
1 cup Amarena or brandied sour cherries in syrup, drained
Turbinado sugar, for sprinkling

Megan Garrelts, pastry chef at Bluestem in Kansas City, Missouri, makes these oversize oatmeal cookies with Amarena cherries in syrup, which give them a wonderfully chewy texture. For a more grown-up recipe, swap in brandied cherries.

1 Preheat the oven to 350° and position racks in the upper and lower thirds. Line 2 large baking sheets with parchment paper.

2 In a medium bowl, whisk both flours with the baking soda, salt, cinnamon and nutmeg. In a large bowl, using a hand mixer, beat the butter with the granulated and brown sugars at medium-high speed until light and fluffy, about 5 minutes. Add the eggs and vanilla and beat until smooth. Add the dry ingredients and beat at low speed until combined. Add the oats and cherries and beat until the cherries are slightly mashed and evenly distributed.

3 Working in batches, scoop 6 scant ¼-cup balls of dough onto each of the prepared baking sheets, spacing them evenly, and sprinkle with turbinado sugar. Bake for 16 minutes, shifting the sheets from top to bottom and front to back halfway through, until dark golden brown. Let the cookies cool on the baking sheets for about 5 minutes, then transfer them to a rack to cool completely. Bake the remaining 6 cookies.

MAKE AHEAD

The cookies can be kept in an airtight container at room temperature for up to 3 days or frozen for up to 1 month.

"If you're a texture junkie like me, you'll love these cookies. Each one is the size of a saucer, so the edges get crumbly-crisp while the middle is underbaked, like cookie dough. It's a great contrast with the chewy bits of candied ginger inside and the crackly dusting of turbinado sugar outside." —SUSAN CHOUNG, BOOKS EDITOR

GINGER MOLASSES COOKIES

MAKES **1 dozen**

TIME **30 min plus cooling**

- 2 **cups all-purpose flour**
- 4½ **tsp. ground ginger**
- 2 **tsp. baking soda**
- 1 **tsp. natural unsweetened cocoa powder**
- 1 **tsp. cinnamon**
- ½ **tsp. ground cardamom**
- ½ **tsp. freshly ground black pepper**
- ½ **tsp. fine sea salt**
- ¾ **cup granulated sugar**
- ¼ **cup packed light brown sugar**
- ⅔ **cup canola oil**
- 1 **large egg**
- ¼ **cup unsulfured molasses**
- ½ **cup candied ginger, cut into ¼-inch dice**
- ½ **cup turbinado sugar, such as Sugar in the Raw**

"Of all our seasonal cookies, we love this one the most," says Erin Patinkin. She and Agatha Kulaga, the duo behind Ovenly in New York City, like to sandwich the oversize cookies with buttercream or crumble them into ice cream.

1 Preheat the oven to 350°. In a medium bowl, whisk the flour with the ground ginger, baking soda, cocoa powder, cinnamon, cardamom, pepper and salt. In a large bowl, whisk the granulated and brown sugars with the oil, egg and molasses. Add the dry ingredients and candied ginger and stir until just combined.

2 Scrape the dough out onto a work surface and pat into a thick disk. Cut the disk into 12 wedges and roll each wedge into a ball. Place the turbinado sugar in a small bowl and roll each ball of dough in the sugar to coat. Arrange the balls 3 inches apart on 2 baking sheets lined with parchment paper.

3 Bake the cookies for 8 to 10 minutes, until just set at the edges; rotate the sheets from top to bottom and front to back halfway through baking. Let the cookies cool on the baking sheets for 10 minutes, then transfer them to a rack to cool completely.

PECAN SANDIES

MAKES **4 dozen**

TIME **50 min plus overnight chilling**

2 **sticks unsalted butter, at room temperature**

⅓ **cup sugar, plus more for sprinkling**

½ **tsp. salt**

1 **tsp. pure vanilla extract**

2 **cups all-purpose flour**

1 **cup pecans, coarsely chopped**

These nutty cookies from cookbook author Angie Mosier are unbelievably light, delicate and crisp. The secret is to let the dough chill overnight before slicing and baking.

1 In a medium bowl, using a hand mixer, beat the butter with the ⅓ cup of sugar and the salt at medium speed until light and fluffy, about 3 minutes. Beat in the vanilla, then beat in the flour at low speed, scraping the sides and bottom of the bowl, until the dough just comes together. Add the pecans and beat just until they are incorporated and lightly broken up. Divide the dough in half and form it into two 2-inch-thick logs. Wrap tightly in plastic and refrigerate overnight.

2 Preheat the oven to 350°. Line 3 baking sheets with parchment paper. Working with 1 log at a time and keeping the other one chilled, cut the dough into scant ¼-inch-thick slices, arrange them on the baking sheets and sprinkle them with sugar. Repeat with the second log of dough.

3 Bake the cookies for 25 to 30 minutes, until lightly golden around the edges and on the bottoms, shifting the baking sheets halfway through. Let the cookies cool on the baking sheets for a few minutes, then transfer them to a rack to cool completely.

MAKE AHEAD

The cookies can be stored in an airtight container for up to 3 days.

"It's awesome when just a few ingredients can turn into something so dreamy. When nutty cookies are done right, they're so addictive! Just a few words of advice: Make sure your pecans are fresh, and don't skip chilling the dough."

—KATE HEDDINGS, EXECUTIVE FOOD EDITOR

PEANUT BUTTER AND JELLY SANDWICH COOKIES

MAKES 1 dozen sandwich cookies

TIME Active 40 min; Total 1 hr 30 min

COOKIES

1½ cups all-purpose flour

1½ tsp. baking soda

¼ tsp. kosher salt

1 stick unsalted butter, at room temperature

½ cup lightly packed light brown sugar

½ cup granulated sugar

1 large egg

½ tsp. pure vanilla extract

½ cup creamy natural peanut butter

¼ cup chopped honey-roasted peanuts

FILLING

⅓ cup creamy natural peanut butter

5 Tbsp. unsalted butter, softened

¼ cup confectioners' sugar

¼ tsp. pure vanilla extract

⅛ tsp. kosher salt

¼ cup seedless jam, such as Concord grape, raspberry or strawberry

Tiffany MacIsaac of Buttercream Bakeshop in Washington, DC, gives her irresistible PB&J sandwich cookies extra nutty crunch by sprinkling honey-roasted peanuts on the dough before baking.

1 MAKE THE COOKIES Preheat the oven to 350°. Line 2 large baking sheets with parchment paper. In a medium bowl, whisk the flour, baking soda and salt. In another medium bowl, using a hand mixer, beat the butter with both sugars at medium speed until light and fluffy, about 3 minutes. Beat in the egg and vanilla, then beat in the dry ingredients in 3 batches, mixing well between additions. Fold in the peanut butter until it is fully incorporated.

2 Scoop 24 one-inch balls of dough onto the baking sheets, at least 2 inches apart. Press the balls down slightly; they should be about 1½ inches in diameter. Sprinkle the tops with the chopped peanuts. Bake the cookies for 10 to 12 minutes, until the edges are light golden brown and the tops are slightly cracked; rotate the baking sheets halfway through. Let the cookies cool for 10 minutes on the baking sheets, then transfer to a rack to cool completely.

3 MEANWHILE, MAKE THE FILLING In a medium bowl, using a hand mixer, whip the peanut butter with the butter, confectioners' sugar, vanilla and salt at medium speed until fluffy, about 5 minutes. Refrigerate for about 45 minutes, until chilled.

4 Spoon 1½ tablespoons of the filling on the underside of 12 cookies. Spread 1 teaspoon of jam on the underside of the remaining cookies. Sandwich the halves together and serve.

MAKE AHEAD

The assembled cookies can be refrigerated for up to 3 days.

HONEY–TAHINI COOKIES

MAKES **30**

TIME **45 min**

½ **cup sesame seeds**

1½ **cups almond flour (see Note)**

½ **tsp. baking soda**

¼ **tsp. sea salt**

⅓ **cup honey**

⅓ **cup tahini**

1 **tsp. vanilla extract**

NOTE

Almond flour, also known as almond meal, is made from finely ground almonds and is available at health food stores.

These chewy-crisp, gluten-free cookies are from Anja Schwerin, a health-conscious cook and food blogger based in Berlin.

1 Preheat the oven to 350° and line 2 baking sheets with parchment paper. Spread the sesame seeds in a pie plate.

2 In a small bowl, whisk the almond flour with the baking soda and salt. In a large bowl, mix the honey with the tahini and vanilla extract. Add the dry ingredients and stir until well incorporated.

3 Using a 1½-inch scoop, scoop the dough into balls. Roll the balls in the sesame seeds, then flatten them into ¼-inch-thick rounds.

Transfer the rounds to the prepared baking sheets, about 2 inches apart.

4 Bake the cookies for about 8 minutes, until the bottoms are golden; shift the pans from top to bottom halfway through. Transfer the cookies to a rack and let cool before serving.

MAKE AHEAD

The cookies can be stored in an airtight container overnight.

"Toasty and not too sweet, these are the thinking person's answer to peanut butter cookies. I roll my dough in black sesame seeds. I love the contrast in color, and maybe I'm just imagining it, but I think the black seeds have a deeper flavor than white ones."

—SUSAN CHOUNG, BOOKS EDITOR

BUTTERY HAZELNUT–FIG BISCOTTI

MAKES   **About 6 dozen**

TIME   **Active 30 min;**
        Total 2 hr plus cooling

2½ cups hazelnuts (10 oz.)

14   oz. dried Calimyrna figs

1½ sticks cold unsalted butter,
     cubed

1¾ cups sugar

 3   large eggs

3½ cups all-purpose flour

 1   Tbsp. baking powder

1½ tsp. salt

"Most biscotti are hard enough to break your teeth," says Julianne Jones of Vergennes Laundry in Vergennes, Vermont. So she came up with this softer version by including a good amount of butter and chewy dried figs.

1 Preheat the oven to 325° and position racks in the upper and lower thirds. Spread the hazelnuts on a baking sheet and toast for 12 to 14 minutes, until the skins blister. Let cool, then transfer the nuts to a kitchen towel and rub off as much of the skins as possible. Transfer the nuts to a cutting board and coarsely chop.

2 Meanwhile, in a microwave-safe bowl, cover the figs with water and microwave at high power for 1 minute, just until plump. Drain well. Trim off the stem ends and slice the figs ⅛ inch thick.

3 In the bowl of a stand mixer fitted with the paddle, beat the butter with the sugar at medium speed until smooth. Beat in the eggs. In a medium bowl, whisk the flour, baking powder and salt. Add the dry ingredients to the butter mixture and beat at low speed until combined. Add the nuts and figs and beat until combined.

4 Line 2 large baking sheets with parchment paper. Transfer the dough to a work surface and roll into six 10-by-1½-inch logs. Arrange the logs on the baking sheets and bake for 30 minutes, until golden and firm. Let the logs cool for 15 minutes.

5 On a work surface, using a serrated knife, slice the logs on the diagonal ⅔ inch thick. Arrange the biscotti cut side up on the baking sheets and bake for about 18 minutes, until lightly browned. Let the biscotti cool, then serve or store.

MAKE AHEAD

The biscotti can be stored in an airtight container for up to 2 weeks.

> "This impossible-to-resist crumble is one of the greatest we've ever tried in the Food & Wine Test Kitchen. We like it so much, we make extra batches and store them in the freezer for snacking on right out of the icebox."
> —KATE HEDDINGS, EXECUTIVE FOOD EDITOR

DOUBLE–CHOCOLATE COOKIE CRUMBLE

MAKES 9 cups

TIME Active 20 min;
Total 50 min plus cooling

- ½ lb. 72% dark chocolate, coarsely chopped
- 1¾ cups all-purpose flour
- ⅓ cup oat flour
- ¼ cup plus 2 Tbsp. unsweetened cocoa powder
- 2 tsp. baking soda
- 1¼ tsp. kosher salt
- 2 sticks unsalted butter, at room temperature
- 1 cup turbinado sugar
- ⅓ cup plus 1 Tbsp. granulated sugar
- Vanilla ice cream, for serving

This addictive cookie crumble from Nicole Krasinski of State Bird Provisions in San Francisco is crisp, light and deeply chocolaty, with a nice saltiness. It's perfect on ice cream but also insanely good on its own.

1 In a food processor, pulse the chocolate until it is the size of peas. Transfer to a plate and freeze for 30 minutes.

2 Preheat the oven to 325°. Line 2 rimmed baking sheets with parchment paper. In a medium bowl, sift both flours with the cocoa powder, baking soda and salt. In a large bowl, using a hand mixer, beat the butter with both sugars at medium speed until very light and fluffy, about 5 minutes. Beat in the flour mixture just until incorporated, then stir in the frozen chocolate.

3 Drop almond-size clumps of dough in a single layer onto the prepared baking sheets; the dough will look crumbly and uneven. Bake until the top is dry but the crumble is still soft, 8 to 10 minutes. Let cool completely. Serve over ice cream.

MAKE AHEAD

The raw dough can be frozen for up to 1 month. The baked crumble can be frozen in a resealable plastic bag for up to 1 month.

MATCHA TEA CAKE COOKIES

MAKES 2 dozen

TIME Active 30 min;
Total 1 hr plus cooling

- 2 cups all-purpose flour
- 2 tsp. baking powder
- ½ tsp. kosher salt
- ⅛ tsp. ground cardamom
- ¾ cup granulated sugar
- ⅔ cup canola oil
- 2 large eggs
- ½ tsp. pure vanilla extract
- ¼ tsp. pure almond extract
- 2 Tbsp. plus 1 tsp. matcha tea powder (see Note)
- ¼ cup confectioners' sugar

NOTE

Matcha is Japanese powdered green tea. It's available at Asian markets, large grocery stores and from amazon.com.

Cookbook author Ben Mims makes these not-too-sweet cookies with a soft, cake-like texture. The "it" ingredient matcha—an antioxidant-rich green tea powder—gives the cookies a beautiful color and a light, toasty flavor.

1 In a medium bowl, whisk the flour, baking powder, salt and cardamom. In another bowl, whisk the granulated sugar, oil, eggs and vanilla and almond extracts. In a small bowl, stir 2 tablespoons of the matcha powder with 2 tablespoons of water, then stir into the wet ingredients. Stir the wet ingredients into the flour mixture just until combined.

2 Line 2 baking sheets with parchment paper. Using a 1-ounce ice cream scoop or 2 tablespoons, scoop 1-inch balls of dough at least 2 inches apart onto the prepared sheets; refrigerate for at least 20 minutes. Meanwhile, preheat the oven to 350°.

3 Bake the cookies for about 10 minutes, until set at the edges and very lightly browned on the bottoms. Let the cookies cool on the sheets for 10 minutes, then transfer to a rack to cool completely.

4 Arrange the cookies on 1 baking sheet. In a sieve, combine the confectioners' sugar with the remaining 1 teaspoon of matcha. Dust over the cookies and serve.

MAKE AHEAD

The cookies can be stored in an airtight container for up to 3 days. Dust with the matcha sugar before serving.

"The sweet grassiness of the green tea powder pairs perfectly with the almond and vanilla, but don't use your super-expensive, hand-carried-from-Japan matcha. Most respected tea companies now sell a less expensive culinary-grade matcha for baking."
—JULIA HEFFELFINGER, ASSOCIATE FOOD EDITOR

SEAWEED SHORTBREAD

MAKES **About 30 cookies**

TIME **Active 25 min;
Total 2 hr plus cooling**

**2 sticks unsalted butter,
softened, plus more for
greasing**

**2 cups plus 2 Tbsp.
all-purpose flour**

½ cup rice flour

½ tsp. kosher salt

**½ cup plus 3 Tbsp. seasoned
roasted seaweed
(kimjaban; see Note)**

**½ cup superfine sugar,
plus more for sprinkling**

**1 large egg beaten with
1 tsp. water**

Flaky sea salt, for sprinkling

NOTE

Kimjaban, a crumbled seaweed
snack seasoned with sesame
oil, salt and sugar, is available at
Asian grocery stores and
online from amazon.com. You can
also use sheets of seasoned
roasted nori.

Cooking Channel host Judy Joo
gives her sweet-and-savory
shortbread bars a pleasant
brininess with an unexpected
ingredient: the seasoned
roasted seaweed called
kimjaban. Seaweed is commonly
used in Asian desserts, like
Korean junbyung cookies.

1 Preheat the oven to 300°. Grease
a 9-inch square baking pan and
line with parchment paper, leaving
a few inches of overhang on
2 sides. Line a rimmed baking
sheet with parchment paper.

2 In a medium bowl, whisk the all-
purpose and rice flours with the
kosher salt. Place the seaweed in
a small resealable plastic bag
and lightly crush with a rolling pin.
Whisk ½ cup of the crushed
seaweed into the dry ingredients.

3 In a large bowl, using a hand mixer,
beat the 2 sticks of butter at
medium-high speed until light
and fluffy, about 2 minutes. Add
the ½ cup of sugar and beat until
the mixture is smooth and pale
yellow, scraping down the sides
of the bowl as needed, about
2 minutes more. Beat in the dry
ingredients; the mixture will
resemble wet sand and hold
together when pressed. Transfer
the dough to the prepared pan
and pat into an even layer. Bake
for about 1 hour and 20 minutes,
until the shortbread is a light
golden brown. Let cool on a rack
for 5 minutes. Leave the oven on.

4 Using the parchment overhang,
transfer the shortbread to a work
surface. Brush the top with the
egg wash and sprinkle with sugar,
flaky sea salt and the remaining
3 tablespoons of crushed seaweed.
Cut the shortbread square into
thirds, then slice crosswise into
¾-inch-wide cookies. Transfer to
the prepared baking sheet and
bake until golden brown on top,
about 10 minutes. Transfer
the cookies to a rack and let cool
completely before serving.

MAKE AHEAD

The cookies can be stored in an
airtight container for up to 1 week.

BILLIONAIRE'S SHORTBREAD

MAKES 16 bars

TIME Active 1 hr;
Total 3 hr 15 min

SHORTBREAD

- 1 stick cold unsalted butter, cubed
- ¾ cup all-purpose flour
- ⅓ cup sugar
- ¼ cup fine cornmeal
- ½ tsp. kosher salt

CARAMEL

- 1 stick unsalted butter
- ½ cup heavy cream
- ½ tsp. kosher salt
- 1 cup sugar

GANACHE

- 9 oz. 70% dark chocolate
- ¾ cup heavy cream
  Flaky sea salt, for garnish
  Mini marshmallows, toasted nuts, thinly sliced candied ginger or crushed pretzels, for topping

To put her own spin on the popular British confection known as Millionaire's Shortbread, NYC pastry chef Jen Yee sprinkles the chocolate ganache layer with flaky sea salt. She encourages bakers to add whatever toppings they prefer: marshmallows, crushed pretzels, candied ginger, toasted nuts—the options are endless.

1 MAKE THE SHORTBREAD Preheat the oven to 350° and line an 8-inch square baking pan with foil, allowing 2 inches of overhang on 2 sides. In a food processor, combine all of the ingredients and pulse until a dough forms, 1 to 2 minutes. Press the dough evenly into the prepared pan. Bake for about 25 minutes, until the shortbread is firm and the edges are golden; let cool completely.

2 MAKE THE CARAMEL In a small saucepan, melt the butter with the cream and salt over moderate heat; keep warm. In a medium saucepan, combine the sugar and 2 tablespoons of water and cook over moderate heat, swirling without stirring, until a golden caramel forms, about 7 minutes. Carefully drizzle in the warm cream and cook over moderate heat, stirring constantly, until the temperature reaches 230° on a candy thermometer, 3 to 5 minutes. Immediately pour the caramel over the cooled shortbread and let cool completely, about 45 minutes.

3 MAKE THE GANACHE Finely chop the chocolate and transfer it to a medium heatproof bowl. In a small saucepan, bring the cream just to a simmer. Immediately pour the hot cream over the chocolate and let stand until the chocolate starts to melt, about 2 minutes; stir until thickened and smooth. Pour the ganache over the cooled caramel and spread it in an even layer with an offset spatula. Sprinkle with flaky sea salt and your choice of toppings and refrigerate until chilled, about 1 hour. Lift the square out of the pan using the long sides of the foil. Cut the shortbread into squares and serve slightly chilled.

MAKE AHEAD

The squares can be refrigerated for up to 3 days. Let stand at room temperature for 30 minutes before serving.

"Macaroons are one of the first things I learned to bake as a kid, and I've loved them ever since. These are moist and chewy on the inside with a bit of toasty crunch on the outside. I sometimes make a larger, flatter version, add a scoop of ice cream and fold it like a taco." —CHRISTINE QUINLAN, DEPUTY EDITOR

COCONUT MACAROONS

MAKES **About 40**

TIME **Active 30 min;**
Total 1 hr plus cooling

One 14-oz. bag sweetened shredded coconut

One 14-oz. can sweetened condensed milk

1 tsp. pure vanilla extract

2 large egg whites

¼ tsp. salt

4 oz. bittersweet chocolate, melted

These sweet and chewy two-bite cookies have only five ingredients (not including the delicious bittersweet chocolate drizzle). Danny Cohen, founder of Danny Macaroons in New York City, doesn't think all macaroons have to be round. "Make whatever shape you want," he says. "There are no rules."

1 Preheat the oven to 350° and line 2 baking sheets with parchment paper. In a medium bowl, combine the coconut with the condensed milk and vanilla. In another bowl, using a hand mixer, beat the egg whites with the salt until firm peaks form. Fold the beaten whites into the coconut mixture.

2 Scoop tablespoon-size mounds of the mixture onto the prepared baking sheets, about 1 inch apart. Bake in the upper and middle thirds of the oven for about 25 minutes, until golden; shift the sheets from top to bottom and front to back halfway through baking. Transfer the baking sheets to racks and let the cookies cool completely.

3 Dip the bottoms of the macaroons into the melted chocolate, letting any excess drip back into the bowl. Return the cookies to the lined baking sheets. Drizzle any remaining chocolate on top and refrigerate for about 5 minutes, until set.

MAKE AHEAD

The macaroons can be refrigerated for up to 2 weeks.

CHOCOLATE CHIP–ESPRESSO MERINGUES

MAKES **8**

TIME **Active 20 min;
Total 1 hr 20 min
plus cooling**

- 3 **large egg whites, at room
temperature**
- ½ **tsp. cream of tartar**
- 1 **cup superfine sugar**
- 2 **oz. bittersweet chocolate,
finely chopped (scant ½ cup)**
  Kosher salt
- 1 **Tbsp. unsweetened
cocoa powder**
- 2 **tsp. espresso powder**

📷 OPPOSITE PAGE

Atlanta pastry chef Abigail Quinn makes these supersize crisp and chewy meringues with just enough espresso and bittersweet chocolate to keep them from being overly sweet.

1 Preheat the oven to 225°. Line a large rimmed baking sheet with parchment paper. In a medium bowl, using a hand mixer, beat the egg whites with the cream of tartar at low speed until foamy, about 30 seconds. Increase the speed to medium and beat in the sugar 1 tablespoon at a time; beat until the whites are stiff and glossy, about 1 minute. Fold in the chopped chocolate and a pinch of salt. Sift the cocoa powder and espresso powder over the meringue and fold 2 or 3 times to incorporate; the meringue should look marbled.

2 Spoon eight ½-cup mounds of meringue onto the prepared baking sheet. Using the back of a spoon, gently spread the meringues into 3-inch rounds. Bake for 1 hour, until the meringues are firm on the outsides but still chewy in the centers. Let cool completely.

ALMOND MERINGUE COOKIES

MAKES **30**

TIME **Active 15 min;
Total 2 hr 15 min
plus cooling**

- ¾ **cup whole raw almonds**
  Nonstick cooking spray
- 4 **cold large egg whites**
- 1 **cup superfine sugar**

Skye McAlpine, the Venice-based author of the blog From My Dining Table, bakes these cookies at a low temperature so the outsides get crisp while the middles stay chewy. You can swap in another nut for the almonds if you prefer.

1 Preheat the oven to 350°. Spread the almonds in a cake pan and bake until lightly toasted, about 8 minutes. Let cool slightly, then coarsely chop. Reduce the oven temperature to 225°.

2 Line 2 rimmed baking sheets with parchment paper and lightly coat with nonstick spray. In a medium bowl, using a hand mixer, beat the egg whites at low speed until foamy. At medium-high speed, beat in the sugar 1 tablespoon at a time; continue beating until glossy, firm peaks form, about 10 minutes. Fold in the toasted almonds.

3 Scoop fifteen 2-tablespoon-size mounds of the meringue onto each of the prepared baking sheets. Bake for 1 hour, until the meringues are firm. Turn the oven off; leave the cookies in for 30 minutes, then transfer to a rack to cool.

CHOCOLATE-OATMEAL CARMELITAS

MAKES **2 dozen bars**

TIME **Active 30 min;
Total 1 hr 20 min plus
overnight resting**

- 4 **sticks (1 lb.) unsalted butter, softened, plus more for greasing**
- 3 **cups plus 3 Tbsp. all-purpose flour**
- 1½ **tsp. baking soda**
- ½ **tsp. salt**
- 3 **cups quick-cooking rolled oats**
- 2¼ **cups light brown sugar**
-   **One 16-oz. jar dulce de leche (1½ cups; see Note)**
- 1½ **cups semisweet chocolate chips**
- ¾ **cup chopped pecans**

NOTE

You can find dulce de leche, the rich, creamy caramel sauce popular in Latin America, at most supermarkets and specialty food shops.

Over the years, Louis Lambert of Lamberts Downtown Barbecue in Austin has fed a lot of politicians (including both Bush presidents). He first made these carmelitas for Lady Bird Johnson, who was hosting a fundraiser at a ranch outside Johnson City. Laced with chocolate, pecans and dulce de leche, these chewy, decadent bar cookies have become one of his most popular recipes.

1 Preheat the oven to 350°. Butter a 9-by-13-inch metal baking pan. In a large bowl, whisk 3 cups of the flour with the baking soda and salt. Add the 4 sticks of butter, the oats and brown sugar and mix until combined. In a small bowl, mix the dulce de leche with the remaining 3 tablespoons of flour.

2 Pat half of the oat mixture into the baking pan. Bake for 15 minutes. Scatter half of the chocolate chips and pecans over the crust. Dollop half of the dulce de leche mixture on top. Crumble the remaining oat mixture evenly into the pan. Cover with the remaining chocolate chips, pecans and dulce de leche. Bake until the edges are set, about 35 minutes. Let stand uncovered at room temperature overnight. Cut the carmelitas into bars and serve.

"These bars are my ultimate comfort food—chocolaty, caramelly, chewy, oaty with just a touch of salt. They are my go-to for bake sales, picnics, care packages, you name it. If you don't have dulce de leche, traditional caramel or butterscotch sauce works well too." —CHRISTINE QUINLAN, DEPUTY EDITOR

CHOCOLATE-PEPPERMINT BROWNIES

MAKES 2 dozen

TIME Active 15 min;
Total 45 min
plus 2 hr cooling

2 **sticks unsalted butter,
cut into small pieces,
plus more for greasing**

1 **lb. bittersweet chocolate,
chopped**

2 **tsp. pure peppermint extract**

4 **large eggs**

1¾ **cups packed light brown sugar**

¾ **cup all-purpose flour**

1 **tsp. fine sea salt**

4 **candy canes, crushed
(⅓ cup)**

Claire Ptak of London's cult-favorite bakery Violet gives her rich brownies a double dose of mint: She stirs peppermint extract into the batter and also tops the bars with crushed candy canes. Can't find candy canes? Use striped peppermint candies instead.

1 Preheat the oven to 350°. Butter a 9-by-13-inch baking pan and line with parchment paper, allowing 2 inches of overhang on the long sides.

2 In a heatproof bowl, combine two-thirds of the chopped chocolate with the 2 sticks of butter. Set the bowl over a pot of simmering water and stir until melted. Scrape the chocolate into another bowl and let cool slightly. Add the remaining chopped chocolate and the peppermint extract to the heatproof bowl and melt over the simmering water; remove from the heat and let cool slightly.

3 In a medium bowl, whisk the eggs with the brown sugar until combined. Whisk in the chocolate-butter mixture until glossy and thick. Sprinkle the flour and salt into the bowl and stir until just incorporated. Spread the brownie batter in the prepared baking pan. Dollop the peppermint chocolate onto the brownie batter and swirl in with a table knife.

4 Bake the brownies in the center of the oven for 15 minutes. Sprinkle the crushed candy canes on top and bake for 10 to 15 minutes longer, until the edges are set and a toothpick inserted in the center comes out with a few moist crumbs. Let the brownies cool in the pan for at least 2 hours. Cut into squares and serve.

"I've loved mint with chocolate ever since I first tasted After Eights at my grandmother's house. This recipe captures that killer flavor combo to a tee. The thin chocolate mints have been replaced by a dense and gooey brownie laced with crunchy bits of candy canes." —KATE HEDDINGS, EXECUTIVE FOOD EDITOR

"I don't like brownies that are too cakey or so fudgy they're the consistency of spackle. These are just right. The salt in the batter highlights the chocolate flavor. I sometimes even sprinkle on a little extra salt after they bake." —SUSAN CHOUNG, BOOKS EDITOR

SALTED FUDGE BROWNIES

MAKES 16

TIME 45 min plus 2 hr cooling

1½ sticks unsalted butter, plus more for greasing

2 oz. unsweetened chocolate, finely chopped

¼ cup plus 2 Tbsp. unsweetened cocoa

2 cups sugar

3 large eggs

1½ tsp. pure vanilla extract

1 cup all-purpose flour

½ tsp. Maldon sea salt

Former F&W restaurant editor Kate Krader has been making these fudgy, sweet-salty brownies since she was 10. As a kid she used regular table salt; now she recommends a flaky sea salt, because the flavor is milder and it melts so nicely into the batter, accentuating the chocolaty sweetness.

1 Preheat the oven to 350°. Line a 9-inch square metal cake pan with foil, draping the foil over the edges. Lightly butter the foil.

2 In a large saucepan, melt the 1½ sticks of butter with the unsweetened chocolate over very low heat, stirring occasionally. Remove from the heat. Whisking them in 1 at a time until thoroughly incorporated, add the cocoa, sugar, eggs, vanilla and flour. Pour the batter into the prepared pan and smooth the surface. Sprinkle the salt evenly over the batter. Using a butter knife, swirl the salt into the batter.

3 Bake the brownies in the center of the oven for about 35 minutes, until the edges are set but the center is still a bit soft and a toothpick inserted into the center comes out coated with a little of the batter. Let the brownies cool at room temperature in the pan for 1 hour, then refrigerate just until firm, about 1 hour. Lift the brownies from the pan and peel off the foil. Cut the brownies into 16 squares and serve at room temperature.

MAKE AHEAD

The brownies can be refrigerated for up to 3 days or frozen for up to 1 month.

BACK-TO-SCHOOL RASPBERRY GRANOLA BARS

MAKES 16

TIME Active 15 min;
Total 1 hr plus 3 hr cooling

- 1½ sticks unsalted butter, melted, plus more for greasing
- 1 cup pecans, coarsely chopped
- 1½ cups all-purpose flour
- 1¼ cups old-fashioned rolled oats
- ⅓ cup granulated sugar
- ⅓ cup packed dark brown sugar
- 1 tsp. kosher salt
- ½ tsp. baking soda
- 1 cup raspberry preserves

Karen DeMasco, pastry chef at Hearth in New York City, makes crumbly soft, jammy-sweet bars that travel well, so they're ideal for school bake sales and lunch boxes. "They're quick to put together with pantry staples, and everyone seems to love them," she says. Substitute any flavor of jam for the raspberry preserves called for here.

1 Preheat the oven to 350°. Butter an 8-inch square baking pan and line the bottom and sides with parchment paper. Spread the pecans in a pie plate and toast for about 5 minutes, until lightly browned and fragrant. Let cool.

2 In a large bowl, whisk the flour with the oats, both sugars, salt, baking soda and pecans. Using a wooden spoon, stir in the melted butter until the oat mixture is thoroughly combined.

3 Press two-thirds of the oat mixture evenly into the bottom of the prepared baking pan. Top with the raspberry preserves, then sprinkle with the remaining oat mixture.

4 Bake for about 45 minutes, rotating the pan halfway through baking, until the top is golden brown. Transfer the pan to a wire rack and let the granola bars cool completely, about 3 hours. Cut into squares and serve.

MAKE AHEAD

The bars can be kept in an airtight container for up to 1 week.

APPLE PIE BARS

MAKES   **4 dozen**

TIME   **Active 1 hr;
Total 2 hr plus cooling**

CRUST

- **3 sticks unsalted butter, softened**
- **¾ cup granulated sugar**
- **3 cups all-purpose flour**
- **½ tsp. kosher salt**

FILLING

- **6 Tbsp. unsalted butter**
- **½ cup light brown sugar**
- **12 Granny Smith apples (about 6 lbs.)—peeled, cored and thinly sliced**
- **1 Tbsp. cinnamon**
- **¼ tsp. freshly grated nutmeg**

TOPPING

- **¾ cup walnuts**
- **3 cups quick-cooking oats**
- **2 cups all-purpose flour**
- **1½ cups light brown sugar**
- **1¼ tsp. cinnamon**
- **½ tsp. baking soda**
- **½ tsp. kosher salt**
- **3 sticks unsalted butter, cut into ½-inch cubes and chilled**

America's most iconic dessert is transformed into an even more indulgent snack in these apple pie bars with a nutty streusel topping and a crisp, buttery shortbread crust. A seasonal specialty of Big Sugar Bakeshop in Los Angeles, the recipe is the brainchild of Cathy Johnson, sister of Big Sugar's Mary Odson.

1 MAKE THE CRUST Preheat the oven to 375°. Line a 15-by-17-inch rimmed baking sheet with parchment paper. In a stand mixer fitted with the paddle, beat the butter with the granulated sugar at medium speed until light and fluffy, 2 minutes. At low speed, beat in the flour and salt until a soft dough forms. Press the dough over the bottom of the sheet and ½ inch up the sides. Bake in the center of the oven for 20 minutes, until the crust is golden. Let cool on a rack. Leave the oven on.

2 MAKE THE FILLING In each of 2 large skillets, melt 3 tablespoons of the butter with ¼ cup of the brown sugar. Add the apples to the skillets and cook over high heat, stirring occasionally, until softened, about 10 minutes. Stir half of the cinnamon and nutmeg into each skillet. Cook until the apples are caramelized and very tender and the liquid has evaporated, about 10 minutes longer; scrape up any bits stuck to the bottom of the skillets and add up to ½ cup of water to each pan to prevent scorching. Let cool.

3 MAKE THE TOPPING Spread the walnuts in a pie plate and toast in the oven until golden and fragrant, about 8 minutes. Let cool, then coarsely chop. In a large bowl, mix the oats with the flour, brown sugar, cinnamon, baking soda and salt. Using a pastry blender or 2 knives, cut in the butter until the mixture resembles coarse meal. Stir in the walnuts and press the mixture into clumps.

4 Spread the apple filling over the crust. Scatter the crumbs on top, pressing them lightly into an even layer. Bake in the center of the oven for about 1 hour, until the topping is golden; rotate the pan halfway through baking. Let cool completely on a rack before cutting into 2-inch bars.

MAKE AHEAD

The bars can be stored in an airtight container at room temperature for 4 days or frozen for up to 1 month.

LEMON-CRANBERRY PIE BARS

MAKES	One 9-by-13-inch pan
TIME	Active 1 hr; Total 1 hr 45 min plus cooling

CRUST

2½ sticks cold unsalted butter, cut into cubes

¼ cup plus 2 Tbsp. light brown sugar

¼ cup plus 2 Tbsp. granulated sugar

2½ cups all-purpose flour sifted with ½ tsp. kosher salt

FILLING

1 cup cranberries

2¾ cups granulated sugar

Pinch of ground cloves

4 large eggs plus 2 egg yolks

1 tsp. finely grated lemon zest plus ½ cup fresh lemon juice

¾ cup all purpose flour

Confectioners' sugar, for dusting

Sarah Jordan of Johnny's Grill in Chicago makes a simple pie alternative. Instead of rolling out the dough, you just press the crust into a baking pan, then fill it with a tangy-sweet lemon curd swirled with cranberry puree. For a pumpkin version, turn the page.

1 MAKE THE CRUST In the bowl of a stand mixer fitted with the paddle, cream the butter with both sugars at medium speed for 2 minutes. At low speed, beat in the sifted flour-and-salt mixture.

2 Preheat the oven to 350°. Line a 9-by-13-inch baking pan with parchment paper, allowing 2 inches of overhang on the long sides. Transfer the dough to the pan and press it over the bottom and 1¼ inches up the sides. (You can cover the dough with plastic wrap and press with the bottom of a measuring cup.) Be sure the corners are not too thick. Refrigerate until firm.

3 Bake the crust for 30 to 35 minutes, until golden brown; halfway through baking, use the back of a spoon to smooth the sides and corners of the crust. Transfer the pan to a rack and let the crust cool before filling. Leave the oven on.

4 MEANWHILE, MAKE THE FILLING In a saucepan, simmer the cranberries with ¼ cup of the granulated sugar, the cloves and ¼ cup of water over moderately low heat until the berries pop and the liquid thickens, about 8 minutes. Transfer to a blender and puree until smooth. Strain and press the puree through a fine sieve set over a bowl and let cool completely.

5 In a medium bowl, whisk the remaining 2½ cups of granulated sugar with the eggs, egg yolks, lemon zest, lemon juice and flour. Mix 1 cup of the lemon filling into the cranberry puree; pour the rest of the lemon filling into the crust. Swirl in the cranberry-lemon mixture. Bake for 35 minutes, until set. Transfer the pan to a rack to cool. Dust with confectioners' sugar and serve.

MAKE AHEAD

The bars can be refrigerated for up to 2 days. Serve chilled or at room temperature.

PUMPKIN PIE BARS

MAKES One 9-by-13-inch pan

TIME Active 45 min; Total 1 hr 45 min plus cooling

CRUST

2½ sticks cold unsalted butter, cut into cubes

¼ cup plus 2 Tbsp. light brown sugar

¼ cup plus 2 Tbsp. granulated sugar

2½ cups all-purpose flour sifted with ½ tsp. kosher salt

FILLING

½ cup granulated sugar

¼ cup dark brown sugar

1 tsp. cinnamon

¼ tsp. ground cloves

¼ tsp. ground ginger

¼ tsp. ground cardamom

¼ tsp. salt

2 large eggs

One 15-oz. can pure pumpkin puree

One 12-oz. can evaporated milk

Crème fraîche, for serving

Chicago chef Sarah Jordan's bars have all the spice and warmth of classic pumpkin pie without all the work of rolling out dough and crimping crusts. They're a fun, surprising way to feed a crowd.

1 MAKE THE CRUST In the bowl of a stand mixer fitted with the paddle, cream the butter with both sugars at medium speed for 2 minutes. At low speed, beat in the sifted flour-and-salt mixture.

2 Preheat the oven to 350°. Line a 9-by-13-inch baking pan with parchment paper, allowing 2 inches of overhang on the long sides. Transfer the dough to the pan and press it over the bottom and 1¼ inches up the sides. (You can cover the dough with plastic wrap and press with the bottom of a measuring cup.) Be sure the corners are not too thick. Refrigerate until firm.

3 Bake the crust for 30 to 35 minutes, until golden brown; halfway through baking, use the back of a spoon to smooth the sides and corners of the crust. Transfer the pan to a wire rack and let the crust cool before filling.

4 MAKE THE FILLING Increase the oven temperature to 425°. In a small bowl, whisk both sugars with the spices and salt. In a medium bowl, whisk the eggs. Whisk in the sugar mixture, then whisk in the pumpkin puree and the evaporated milk until smooth.

5 Pour the filling into the crust and bake for 10 minutes. Lower the oven temperature to 350° and bake for about 25 minutes longer, until the filling is fully set. Transfer the pan to a rack and let cool completely. Cut into bars and serve with crème fraîche.

MAKE AHEAD

The pumpkin pie bars can be refrigerated for up to 2 days. Serve chilled or at room temperature.

S'MORES BARS WITH MARSHMALLOW MERINGUE

MAKES 1 dozen

TIME Active 50 min;
Total 2 hr

CRUST

- 3 cups graham cracker crumbs (12 oz.)
- 1½ sticks unsalted butter, melted
- 2 Tbsp. packed light brown sugar
- ¼ tsp. fine sea salt

BROWNIE FILLING

- 1 stick cold unsalted butter, cubed
- 4 oz. unsweetened chocolate, chopped
- 1¼ cups granulated sugar
- 2 tsp. pure vanilla extract
- ¼ tsp. fine sea salt
- 2 large eggs, at room temperature
- ½ cup all-purpose flour

MERINGUE

- 3 large egg whites
- ¾ cup granulated sugar
- ½ tsp. pure vanilla extract
- ¼ tsp. cream of tartar

Be the star of your next potluck with these crazy-delicious bars from Cheryl and Griffith Day of Back in the Day Bakery in Savannah, Georgia. They feature a salty, crunchy graham cracker crust, a rich chocolate filling and a dreamy, mile-high meringue topping.

1 MAKE THE CRUST Preheat the oven to 350°. Line a 9-inch square baking pan with foil, allowing 2 inches of overhang on 2 sides. In a medium bowl, using a fork, mix all of the ingredients until evenly moistened. Press the crumbs evenly into the bottom of the prepared pan. Bake for 8 to 10 minutes, just until lightly browned. Let cool completely. Leave the oven on.

2 MAKE THE FILLING In a medium heatproof bowl set over a saucepan of simmering water, melt the butter with the chocolate over moderate heat, stirring occasionally, until smooth, about 5 minutes. Remove from the heat and whisk in the granulated sugar, vanilla and salt. Whisk in the eggs until smooth, then stir in the flour until just incorporated. Spread the batter evenly over the cooled crust. Bake for about 25 minutes, until the edges are set but the center is still slightly jiggly. Transfer the baking pan to a rack and let cool completely.

3 MAKE THE MERINGUE Preheat the broiler. In a medium heatproof bowl set over a saucepan of simmering water, whisk the egg whites with the granulated sugar until the whites are warm and the sugar is dissolved, about 3 minutes. Transfer the egg whites to the bowl of a stand mixer fitted with the whisk. Add the vanilla and cream of tartar and beat at medium speed until firm. Increase the speed to high and beat the meringue until stiff and glossy, 5 to 7 minutes.

4 Mound the meringue on top of the filling, swirling it decoratively. Broil the meringue 8 inches from the heat until lightly browned at the tips, about 1 minute. Cut into bars and serve.

MAKE AHEAD

The bars can be refrigerated for up to 2 days.

Puddings
& Custards

POPCORN PUDDING

SERVES 6

TIME   30 min plus 2 hr chilling

2¼ cups whole milk

¾ cup heavy cream

½ cup sugar

¼ tsp. salt

 1 tsp. vegetable oil

¼ cup plus 1 Tbsp. popcorn
    kernels

 3 large egg yolks

 4 tsp. cornstarch

 3 Tbsp. unsalted butter, cubed

¼ tsp. pure vanilla extract

It's hard to improve on the creamy indulgence of puddings and custards, but chef Jonathon Sawyer of Cleveland's Greenhouse Tavern does just that. He created this luscious dessert to brilliantly play off the flavor of salted popcorn with the sweetness of vanilla pudding.

1 In a large saucepan, combine the milk, cream, sugar and salt and bring to a boil over moderate heat, stirring to dissolve the sugar. Remove from the heat.

2 In a medium pot, heat the oil. Add the popcorn kernels, cover and cook over moderate heat until they start popping. Cook, shaking the pot constantly, until the popping has almost stopped, 2 to 3 minutes. Pour all but 1 cup of the popcorn into the cream mixture, cover and let stand for 10 minutes. Reserve the remaining popcorn for garnish.

3 In a medium bowl, whisk the egg yolks with the cornstarch until smooth. Strain the hot cream mixture into a clean medium saucepan; discard the solids. Bring the cream to a boil over moderate heat. Gradually whisk 1 cup of the hot cream into the egg yolks, then scrape the mixture into the saucepan. Whisk the pudding over moderate heat until it just comes to a boil, about 2 minutes. Stir in the butter and vanilla.

4 Scrape the pudding into a medium baking dish. Press a piece of plastic wrap directly onto the surface of the pudding and refrigerate until chilled, at least 2 hours. Spoon into bowls, sprinkle with the reserved popcorn and serve.

> "I'm crazy about these lime leaf–scented puddings! They not only taste amazing, but the technique is so cool. Bryant Ng nailed the proper ratio of citrus juice to heavy cream, so they set up brilliantly without any gelatin."
>
> —JUSTIN CHAPPLE, TEST KITCHEN DEPUTY EDITOR

KAFFIR LIME CUSTARDS

SERVES **8**

TIME **30 min plus 2 hr chilling**

- **3½ cups heavy cream**
- **1 cup sugar**
- **2 kaffir lime leaves (see Note)**
- **½ cup plus 2 Tbsp. fresh lime juice**
- **2 tsp. finely grated lime zest**
- **¼ tsp. salt**
- **Sweetened whipped cream, quartered lychees, chopped mint and sea salt, for garnish**

NOTE

Kaffir lime leaves, popular in Indonesian, Thai and other Southeast Asian cuisines, are readily available at specialty food stores and from amazon.com.

This dreamy custard from Bryant Ng of Cassia in L.A. is super silky and astonishingly simple to make. The secret? It firms up in a couple of hours with lime juice instead of the usual eggs or gelatin.

1 In a medium saucepan, combine the heavy cream with the sugar and kaffir lime leaves and bring to a simmer. Cook over moderately low heat, stirring occasionally, until the cream is slightly reduced, about 15 minutes.

2 Whisk the lime juice into the hot cream. Strain the cream through a fine sieve set over a large heatproof measuring cup. Stir in the lime zest and salt. Pour the cream into eight 6-ounce glasses and refrigerate for at least 2 hours, until chilled and set. Top the custards with whipped cream, garnish with lychees, mint and sea salt and serve right away.

MAKE AHEAD

The custards can be refrigerated overnight. Garnish them just before serving.

PETITS POTS À L'ABSINTHE

SERVES **6**

TIME **20 min plus 6 hr chilling**

- 1 **cup heavy cream**
- ⅔ **cup whole milk**
- 2½ **Tbsp. sugar**
- 1 **tsp. unflavored powdered gelatin dissolved in 2 Tbsp. water**
- 1½ **Tbsp. absinthe**

   Fresh berries, for serving

"People always think Didier is a bit of an outlaw because he is obsessed with absinthe," says Julianne Jones about her husband, Didier Murat. The herbal spirit adds a subtle anise flavor to these puddings, which the couple serve at Vergennes Laundry, their laundromat-turned-bakery in Vergennes, Vermont.

1 In a medium saucepan, combine the cream, milk and sugar and bring to a simmer. Off the heat, whisk in the gelatin and absinthe.

2 Strain the mixture into a pitcher and pour into six 4-ounce ramekins or bowls. Press a piece of plastic wrap directly onto the surface of the puddings and refrigerate until set, at least 6 hours. Serve topped with fresh berries.

MAKE AHEAD

The pots à l'absinthe can be refrigerated for up to 3 days.

GOO GOO PIE PARFAITS

SERVES **8**

TIME **1 hr plus 3 hr chilling**

CRÉMEUX

14 oz. milk chocolate,
finely chopped (3 cups)

3½ oz. dark chocolate,
finely chopped (¾ cup)

2 large egg yolks

¼ cup sugar

1 cup whole milk

1 cup heavy cream

PEANUT-CARAMEL SAUCE

½ cup heavy cream

2 Tbsp. unsalted butter

1 cup sugar

1½ Tbsp. light corn syrup

2 Tbsp. whiskey

1 cup salted roasted peanuts
(5 oz.)

Flaky sea salt, whipped
cream and grated chocolate,
for garnish

Rebecca Masson, pastry chef at Fluff Bake Bar in Houston, is known for reimagining childhood sweets with exquisite French technique. Case in point: this over-the-top combination of chocolate crémeux (pudding) and salty caramel-peanut sauce, inspired by the classic Goo Goo Cluster candy bar.

1 MAKE THE CRÉMEUX In a large bowl, combine the 2 chocolates. In a medium bowl, whisk the egg yolks with the sugar until well combined.

2 In a medium saucepan, bring the milk and cream just to a simmer. Whisking constantly, slowly drizzle half of the hot milk into the egg mixture. Pour the milk-egg mixture into the saucepan and cook over low heat, stirring constantly, until the custard is thickened enough to coat the back of a wooden spoon, 12 to 14 minutes. Strain the custard into the bowl of chocolate. Stir until the chocolate is melted and the crémeux is smooth. Spoon into eight 8-ounce glasses or jars. Chill until set, about 3 hours.

3 MEANWHILE, MAKE THE SAUCE In a small saucepan, warm the cream and butter over moderate heat until the butter melts; remove from the heat. In a large saucepan, combine the sugar with the corn syrup and ¼ cup of water and bring to a boil. Cook over moderate heat, swirling the pan occasionally, until the sugar dissolves and a golden amber caramel forms, about 10 minutes. Carefully pour in the cream mixture (it will bubble vigorously) and whisk until smooth. Let the sauce cool to room temperature, about 1 hour. Stir in the whiskey and peanuts.

4 To serve, spoon the peanut-caramel sauce over the crémeux and garnish with sea salt, whipped cream and grated chocolate.

PREP AHEAD

The peanut-caramel sauce and crémeux can be refrigerated in separate containers for up to 3 days. Allow both to come to room temperature before assembling.

FLAN DE CARAMELO

SERVES **8**

TIME **Active 30 min; Total 1 hr 30 min plus 2 hr chilling**

CARAMEL

- **1 cup sugar**
- **2 Tbsp. light corn syrup**
- **2 Tbsp. fresh orange juice plus 1 Tbsp. finely grated orange zest**

CUSTARD

- **1½ cups milk**
- **1½ cups heavy cream**
- **3 large eggs plus 2 large egg yolks**
- **⅔ cup sugar**
- **1 Tbsp. finely grated orange zest**
- **1½ tsp. pure vanilla extract**
- **Kosher salt**

Bizarre Foods host Andrew Zimmern elevates this traditional Spanish dessert to new heights with the simple addition of orange juice and zest.

1 MAKE THE CARAMEL In a small saucepan, gently stir the sugar with the corn syrup, orange juice and 2 tablespoons of water. Bring to a boil over moderate heat. Cook, without stirring, until an amber caramel forms, 6 to 8 minutes. Brush down the sides of the pan with a wet pastry brush if crystals form. Remove the pan from the heat and swirl in the orange zest. Working quickly, pour the caramel into eight 6-ounce ramekins, tilting to coat the bottoms.

2 MAKE THE CUSTARD Preheat the oven to 350°. In a medium saucepan, combine the milk and cream and cook over moderate heat until the temperature reaches 160° on a candy thermometer, 5 to 7 minutes. Meanwhile, in a large heatproof bowl, whisk the whole eggs with the egg yolks, sugar, orange zest, vanilla extract and a pinch of salt. While whisking constantly, slowly add the hot milk mixture to the eggs. Strain the custard through a fine-mesh sieve set over a large heatproof measuring cup.

3 Line a roasting pan with a kitchen towel and set the ramekins on the towel. Pour the custard into the ramekins. Add enough boiling water to the roasting pan to reach halfway up the sides of the ramekins.

4 Loosely tent the pan with foil and bake the flans for 35 to 40 minutes, until just set but still jiggly in the centers. Using tongs, carefully transfer the ramekins to a rack and let the flans cool to room temperature. Cover with plastic wrap and refrigerate for at least 2 hours or, preferably, overnight.

5 Run a thin knife around each flan. Invert a plate over each ramekin, then turn the flan out onto the plate, shaking the ramekin gently if necessary. Serve immediately.

MAKE AHEAD

The flans can be wrapped in plastic and refrigerated for up to 4 days.

PANNA COTTA WITH BERRY GRANITA AND CARAMEL

SERVES 8

TIME 1 hr 30 min plus overnight chilling and freezing

STRAWBERRY GRANITA

- 1 lb. strawberries, hulled and quartered (4 cups)
- ½ cup sugar

PANNA COTTA

- 1 Tbsp. powdered gelatin
- 4 cups heavy cream
- 3 Tbsp. sugar
- 1½ vanilla beans, split and seeds scraped

CARAMEL SAUCE

- 1 cup sugar
- 1 cup heavy cream
- 1 stick unsalted butter, cut into tablespoons and at room temperature
- Kosher salt

MILK CRUMBLE

- ½ cup powdered milk
- ½ cup all-purpose flour
- ¼ cup sugar
- 6 Tbsp. unsalted butter, at room temperature

This voluptuous panna cotta is delightful enough to eat on its own. But at Wildair in New York City, chefs Jeremiah Stone and Fabián von Hauske gild the lily with icy, refreshing strawberry granita, buttery caramel sauce and crunchy bits of milk cookies.

1 MAKE THE STRAWBERRY GRANITA In a blender, puree the strawberries, sugar and ¼ cup plus 2 tablespoons of water until smooth. Scrape into a 9-by-13-inch metal baking pan and freeze overnight.

2 MEANWHILE, MAKE THE PANNA COTTA In a small bowl, whisk the gelatin with ¼ cup plus 2 tablespoons of water until smooth; let stand for 2 minutes. In a medium saucepan, combine 2 cups of the cream with the sugar and vanilla seeds and bring to a simmer, whisking to dissolve the sugar. Add the softened gelatin and cook over moderately low heat, stirring, until the gelatin is dissolved. Remove the pan from the heat and stir in the remaining 2 cups of cream. Pour the panna cotta into eight 6-ounce ramekins, then cover and refrigerate until set, at least 6 hours or overnight.

3 MAKE THE CARAMEL SAUCE In a large skillet, melt the sugar over low heat, swirling the skillet occasionally, until an amber caramel forms, 7 to 8 minutes. Add the cream and butter (the caramel will seize) and cook, stirring occasionally, until the caramel is smooth, about 5 minutes. Scrape into a heatproof bowl, stir in a pinch of salt and let cool to room temperature.

4 MAKE THE MILK CRUMBLE Preheat the oven to 350°. Line a baking sheet with parchment paper. In a medium bowl, combine all of the ingredients, using your fingertips to blend in the butter until clumps form. Transfer to the baking sheet and bake for about 15 minutes, until golden and crisp. Transfer to a rack to cool.

5 To serve, scrape the granita with a fork until icy and flaky. Invert the ramekins onto plates and unmold. Spoon some of the caramel sauce over each panna cotta and top with some of the granita. Garnish with some of the milk crumble and serve.

PREP AHEAD

The granita can be frozen for up to 1 week. The milk crumble can be stored in an airtight container for 3 days. The panna cotta and caramel sauce can be refrigerated separately for 2 days. Just reheat the caramel slightly before serving.

CHIA-SEED PUDDING

SERVES **4**

TIME **15 min plus 4 hr chilling**

2½ cups almond milk

 3 Tbsp. agave nectar

½ cup chia seeds (3 oz.)

½ tsp. finely grated lemon zest

📷 OPPOSITE PAGE

Grace Parisi, author of *Get Saucy,* created this good-for-you dessert by combining just four ingredients, including the nutritional powerhouse chia seeds. As the seeds soak in almond milk, they create a tapioca-like pudding.

In a 1-quart jar, combine the almond milk and agave nectar. Close the jar and shake to combine. Add the chia seeds and lemon zest, then close the jar and shake well. Refrigerate until the mixture is very thick and pudding-like, at least 4 hours or overnight, shaking or stirring occasionally. Serve the pudding in bowls.

SERVE WITH

Diced mango, almonds, citrus sections and extra agave nectar.

MAKE AHEAD

The pudding can be refrigerated for up to 3 days.

GIANDUJA MOUSSE

SERVES **4**

TIME **Active 10 min;
       Total 30 min**

½ cup chocolate-hazelnut paste, such as Nutella

¼ cup crème fraîche

1½ tsp. brandy or hazelnut liqueur

½ cup heavy cream

Chocolate wafer cookies, for serving

As if the chocolate-hazelnut spread gianduja weren't delicious enough straight off the spoon, cookbook author Grace Parisi folds in whipped cream and crème fraîche to create a truly decadent (and ridiculously easy) mousse. For an unforgettable ice cream sandwich, spoon the mousse between chocolate wafers and freeze overnight.

In a medium bowl, using a hand mixer, beat the chocolate-hazelnut paste with the crème fraîche and brandy at low speed until smooth. In another bowl, beat the heavy cream until firm peaks form. Using a rubber spatula, fold the whipped cream into the chocolate-hazelnut mixture until no streaks remain. Spoon the mousse into small bowls and refrigerate for 20 minutes. Serve with chocolate wafer cookies.

"This sweet, custardy pudding could well be the ultimate comfort dessert. There's no pretension here; it's just a bowl of chopped ripe bananas topped with vanilla pudding and a cinnamon-spiked crumble made with always-perfect Nilla Wafers from the supermarket." —KATE HEDDINGS, EXECUTIVE FOOD EDITOR

BANANA PUDDING WITH VANILLA WAFER CRUMBLE

SERVES **6**

TIME **45 min plus 4 hr chilling**

- 5 **large egg yolks**
- ¼ **cup cornstarch**
- ½ **cup plus 2 tsp. sugar**
  Salt
- 2 **cups whole milk**
- 3 **Tbsp. banana liqueur (optional)**
- 2 **Tbsp. cold unsalted butter plus 1 Tbsp. melted butter**
- 2 **tsp. pure vanilla extract**
- 1 **cup vanilla wafer cookies (about 15), coarsely ground**
- ¼ **tsp. cinnamon**
- 2 **ripe bananas, coarsely chopped**

David Guas of DC's Bayou Bakery remembers the consoling powers of this dessert from the buffet spreads at family funerals back home in New Orleans.

1 In a medium bowl, whisk the egg yolks with the cornstarch, ½ cup of the sugar and ¼ teaspoon of salt. In a medium saucepan, bring the milk to a boil. Gradually whisk the hot milk into the egg yolks until smooth. Transfer the pudding mixture to the saucepan and add the banana liqueur. Cook over moderate heat, whisking, until the pudding is thick, about 3 minutes. Scrape the pudding into a bowl and whisk in the cold butter and vanilla. Press a piece of plastic wrap directly onto the surface of the pudding and refrigerate until chilled, about 4 hours.

2 Preheat the oven to 325°. Line a baking sheet with parchment paper. In a bowl, combine the wafers, cinnamon, the remaining 2 teaspoons of sugar and a pinch of salt. Stir in the melted butter. Spread the crumble on the prepared baking sheet; bake for 15 minutes, until lightly browned. Let cool.

3 Spoon the chopped bananas into bowls. Top with the pudding, sprinkle with the crumble and serve right away.

BLOOD ORANGE PANNA COTTA PARFAITS

SERVES **8**

TIME **Active 25 min; Total 50 min plus 5 hr chilling**

PANNA COTTA

1¼ cups fresh blood orange juice, strained

1 cup sugar

2 tsp. unflavored powdered gelatin

2 Tbsp. cold water

3½ cups heavy cream

GELÉE

1 tsp. unflavored powdered gelatin

1 Tbsp. cold water

1¼ cups fresh blood orange juice, strained

¼ cup plus 2 Tbsp. sugar

These Instagram-worthy parfaits—creamy, luscious, bright and tart all at once—have a flavor reminiscent of a Creamsicle. Valerie Gordon of Valerie Confections in L.A. showcases blood orange in both the panna cotta and the thin layer of gelée on top.

1 MAKE THE PANNA COTTA In a medium saucepan, combine the blood orange juice with 2 tablespoons of the sugar and cook over moderately high heat, stirring occasionally with a wooden spoon, until the juice is reduced to ⅔ cup, about 12 minutes. Meanwhile, in a small bowl, sprinkle the gelatin over the cold water and let stand until softened, about 10 minutes.

2 Add the softened gelatin to the reduced juice along with the cream and the remaining ¾ cup plus 2 tablespoons of sugar. Cook over moderately low heat, stirring occasionally, until the gelatin has melted, about 5 minutes; do not let the mixture boil. Ladle the panna cotta mixture into 8 small glasses (about ⅔ cup in each) and refrigerate until firm and set, at least 3 hours.

3 MAKE THE GELÉE In a small bowl, sprinkle the gelatin over the cold water and let stand until softened, about 5 minutes. In a medium saucepan, combine the blood orange juice with the sugar and softened gelatin and cook over moderately low heat, stirring occasionally, until the gelatin has melted, about 3 minutes; do not let the mixture boil. Let cool for 10 minutes.

4 Carefully spoon the gelée over the panna cotta layer (about 3 tablespoons in each glass). Cover and refrigerate the parfaits until the gelée is set, about 2 hours.

MAKE AHEAD

The parfaits can be refrigerated for up to 2 days.

BANANA AND CHOCOLATE CREAM PIE PARFAITS

SERVES 6

TIME **Active 45 min; Total 1 hr 45 min**

PUDDING

- ¼ cup plus 1 Tbsp. cornstarch
- ½ cup sugar
- 1 Tbsp. light corn syrup
- ¼ tsp. kosher salt
- ¼ cup plus 2 Tbsp. unsweetened cocoa powder
- 1½ oz. bittersweet chocolate, finely chopped
- 1 Tbsp. unsalted butter

CRUMBS

- 9 whole graham crackers, coarsely crushed
- 2 Tbsp. unsalted butter, melted
- 2 tsp. honey
- ½ tsp. cinnamon
  Pinch of kosher salt

BANANA CREAM

- 1 cup heavy cream
- ⅓ cup sugar
- ¼ cup mashed banana
- ½ vanilla bean, split and seeds scraped
- 2 sliced bananas and 1 pint banana or vanilla ice cream, for serving

To make her outstanding deconstructed banana cream pie, pastry chef Michelle Karr-Ueoka of Honolulu's MW Restaurant layers chocolate pudding with cinnamon-flavored graham cracker crumbs, ice cream, bananas and banana whipped cream.

1 MAKE THE PUDDING In a small bowl, whisk the cornstarch with ½ cup of water. In a medium saucepan, combine the sugar, corn syrup and salt with 1½ cups of water and bring to a boil. Whisk in the cocoa powder, then whisk in the cornstarch slurry and cook until thick, about 1 minute. Remove from the heat and whisk in the chocolate and butter until smooth. Scrape the pudding into a bowl and press a piece of plastic wrap directly on the surface. Let cool, then refrigerate until chilled, about 1 hour.

2 MEANWHILE, MAKE THE CRUMBS In a medium bowl, toss the crushed graham crackers with the butter, honey, cinnamon and salt until evenly moistened.

3 MAKE THE BANANA CREAM In a large bowl, using a hand mixer, beat the cream with the sugar, mashed banana and vanilla seeds to stiff peaks.

4 Spoon the pudding into six 8-ounce glasses or jars. Top with a sprinkling of the graham cracker crumbs, a layer of sliced bananas and a scoop of ice cream. Garnish the parfaits with a dollop of the banana cream and graham cracker crumbs and serve.

PREP AHEAD

The pudding can be refrigerated for up to 3 days. The graham cracker crumbs can be stored in an airtight container for up to 3 days.

LEMON-BLUEBERRY CHEESECAKE PARFAITS

SERVES **8**

TIME **Active 1 hr;
Total 4 hr**

SHORTBREAD

1¾ cups all-purpose flour

¼ cup plus 2 Tbsp. cornmeal

1 tsp. salt

2 sticks unsalted butter, at room
temperature

¾ cup confectioners' sugar

2 tsp. finely grated orange zest

1 tsp. pure vanilla extract

BLUEBERRY COMPOTE

2 cups blueberries (12 oz.)

¼ cup granulated sugar

¼ cup water

1 tsp. fresh lemon juice

CHEESECAKE CUSTARD

1 cup whole milk

5 Tbsp. granulated sugar

4 large egg yolks

2½ Tbsp. cornstarch

6 oz. cream cheese, at room
temperature

¼ cup plus 2 Tbsp. fresh
lemon juice

1 tsp. finely grated lemon zest,
plus extra strips for garnish

1 tsp. pure vanilla extract

1 cup heavy cream

The late great San Francisco pastry chef Maggie Leung's reimagined cheesecake has three components: creamy custard, crunchy cornmeal shortbread and fresh blueberry compote.

1 MAKE THE SHORTBREAD In a medium bowl, mix the flour with the cornmeal and salt. In a stand mixer fitted with the paddle, mix the butter with the confectioners' sugar at medium speed until creamy, about 2 minutes. Beat in the orange zest and vanilla extract. Add the flour mixture and beat at low speed until the dough just comes together. Pat the shortbread dough into a disk, wrap in plastic and refrigerate for 1 hour.

2 Preheat the oven to 350°. Line 2 large rimmed baking sheets with parchment paper. Unwrap the chilled dough and roll it out between 2 sheets of parchment paper to an 8-inch round, ½ inch thick. Cut the dough into ½-inch-wide strips and transfer to the baking sheets; leave 1 inch between each strip. Refrigerate the dough strips until chilled, 30 minutes.

3 Bake the shortbread for about 20 minutes, until golden; rotate the pans halfway through. While the warm shortbread strips are still on the baking sheet, cut them into ½-inch cubes. Let cool, about 30 minutes.

4 MAKE THE COMPOTE In a small saucepan, combine 1 cup of the berries with the sugar and water.

Bring to a simmer and cook over moderate heat until the blueberries break down, about 5 minutes. Scrape the blueberry sauce into a blender, add the lemon juice and puree until smooth. Scrape the blueberry sauce into a bowl and fold in the remaining 1 cup of whole blueberries. Refrigerate until chilled, about 2 hours.

5 MEANWHILE, MAKE THE CUSTARD In a medium saucepan, bring ¾ cup of the milk to a boil with 3 tablespoons of the sugar; remove from the heat. In a medium bowl, whisk the egg yolks with the cornstarch and the remaining ¼ cup of milk and 2 tablespoons of sugar. Gradually whisk the hot milk into the egg yolks, then pour the mixture into the saucepan; whisk constantly over moderate heat until thickened, about 2 minutes. Over low heat, whisk in the cream cheese, lemon juice, grated lemon zest and vanilla extract until smooth, about 1 minute. Scrape the cheesecake custard into a bowl. Press a piece of plastic wrap directly onto the surface of the custard and refrigerate until chilled, about 2 hours.

6 In a medium bowl, using a hand mixer, beat the cream to medium peaks. Fold the whipped cream into the chilled custard until no streaks remain. Spoon the shortbread cubes and custard into bowls. Drizzle with the compote, garnish with lemon zest strips and serve.

PISTACHIO PAVLOVA
WITH RHUBARB CREAM

SERVES **8**

TIME **Active 40 min; Total 3 hr 15 min plus cooling**

PAVLOVA

- **1 cup chopped unsalted pistachios**
- **2 Tbsp. cornstarch**
- **5 large egg whites, at room temperature**
- **½ tsp. kosher salt**
- **1 tsp. distilled white vinegar**
- **1½ cups sugar**

RHUBARB CREAM

- **4 oz. rhubarb, chopped into 1-inch pieces (1 cup)**
- **¼ cup sugar**
- **½ tsp. finely grated lemon zest plus 3 Tbsp. fresh lemon juice**
- **1 cup hulled and quartered strawberries, plus ½ cup small strawberries for garnish**
- **1 tsp. vanilla bean paste or pure vanilla extract**
- **1½ cups heavy cream, chilled**
- **½ cup mascarpone cheese, chilled**
- **¼ cup chopped unsalted pistachios, for garnish**

Baker Gesine Bullock-Prado, author of *Let Them Eat Cake*, puts a spring spin on the traditional pavlova, folding pistachios into the crisp-chewy meringue and mixing tangy rhubarb and strawberries into the cream that's piled on top.

1 MAKE THE PAVLOVA Preheat the oven to 350°. Line a baking sheet with parchment paper. In a small bowl, toss the pistachios with the cornstarch.

2 In a stand mixer fitted with the whisk, beat the egg whites with the salt at high speed until foamy, 2 minutes. Beat in the vinegar, then beat in the sugar, 1 tablespoon at a time, and continue beating until the whites are glossy and stiff peaks form, 8 to 10 minutes. Gently fold in the pistachio mixture. Using a large spoon, dollop the meringue onto the prepared sheet and spread into a 10-inch round with a slight indentation in the center. Lower the oven temperature to 225° and bake the meringue for about 1½ hours, until crisp but still chewy on the inside. Turn the oven off; let the meringue rest in the oven for 1 hour. Transfer to a rack and let cool.

3 MEANWHILE, MAKE THE RHUBARB CREAM In a small saucepan, simmer the rhubarb with the sugar, lemon zest and lemon juice over moderate heat, stirring and mashing the rhubarb with the back of a wooden spoon, until the sugar is dissolved and the rhubarb breaks down, about 5 minutes. Remove the saucepan from the heat and stir in the quartered strawberries and vanilla bean paste. Let cool completely.

4 In a large bowl, using a hand mixer, beat the heavy cream with the mascarpone at medium speed until moderately firm, about 3 minutes. Stir ¼ cup of the whipped cream into the cooled rhubarb, then fold the mixture into the remaining whipped cream. Spoon the rhubarb cream into the center of the meringue. Garnish with the small strawberries and chopped pistachios and serve.

Frozen Desserts

VANILLA-ALMOND ICE CREAM
WITH CHERRIES AND PISTACHIOS

MAKES **About 1 qt**

TIME **45 min plus 8 hr freezing, then 6 hr freezing**

- 6 large egg yolks
- 1½ cups heavy cream
- 1½ cups whole milk
- ¾ cup sugar
- ¾ tsp. kosher salt
- 1 vanilla bean, split and seeds scraped
- ½ tsp. pure almond extract
- ¾ cup fresh cherries, pitted and halved
- ¼ cup shelled pistachios, coarsely chopped

NOTE

For a decadent twist, instead of cherries and pistachios, try folding in 1 cup of chopped chocolate-covered pretzels or chopped halvah.

Frozen desserts like homemade ice cream are always a hit, but what if you don't have a machine? Try this cheater's method for making ice cream from Justin Chapple, star of F&W's Mad Genius Tips video series. He pours the custard base into a resealable plastic bag, freezes it flat, then pulses it in a food processor until smooth.

1 Set a medium bowl in a large bowl of ice water. In another medium bowl, beat the egg yolks until pale, 1 to 2 minutes.

2 In a medium saucepan, whisk the cream with the milk, sugar, salt and the vanilla bean and seeds. Bring to a simmer, whisking, until the sugar is completely dissolved. Very gradually whisk half of the hot cream mixture into the beaten egg yolks in a thin stream, then whisk this mixture into the saucepan. Cook over moderately low heat, stirring constantly with a wooden spoon, until the custard is thick enough to lightly coat the back of the spoon, about 12 minutes; don't let it boil.

3 Strain the custard through a medium-mesh strainer into the bowl set in the ice water; discard the vanilla bean. Let the custard cool completely, stirring occasionally. Stir in the almond extract. Pour into a large resealable freezer bag and seal, pressing out the air. Lay the bag flat in the freezer and freeze until firm, at least 8 hours or overnight.

4 Working quickly, in batches if necessary, transfer the frozen custard to a food processor. Pulse for 5 seconds at a time until smooth. Transfer the custard to a chilled 9-by-4-inch metal loaf pan and fold in the cherries and pistachios. Cover with plastic wrap and freeze until firm, about 6 hours or overnight.

MAKE AHEAD

The ice cream can be frozen for up to 1 week.

MAPLE SEMIFREDDO
WITH CANDIED PECANS

SERVES **6**

TIME **1 hr 15 min plus 4 hr freezing**

½ **cup pure maple syrup, preferably grade B**

½ **vanilla bean, split and seeds scraped**

1¾ **cups heavy cream**

1 **large egg plus 4 large egg yolks**

¾ **tsp. kosher salt**

¼ **cup maple sugar**

1 **cup candied pecans**

New York City pastry chef Kierin Baldwin makes this insanely delicious, maple-flavored semifreddo (Italian for "half-cold") in a stand mixer. The soft ice cream–like dessert is light, fluffy and super creamy.

1 Fill a large bowl with ice and water. In a medium saucepan, combine the maple syrup with the vanilla bean and seeds and bring to a boil. Cook over moderate heat, stirring occasionally, until extremely fragrant, chocolate brown in color and thickened, 3 to 5 minutes. Remove the pan from the heat. Whisking constantly, slowly drizzle in the heavy cream. Scrape the maple cream into a medium metal bowl and set it in the ice bath; stir occasionally until very cold, about 30 minutes. Discard the vanilla bean. Refrigerate the maple cream.

2 Meanwhile, in the bowl of a stand mixer fitted with the whisk, beat the egg, egg yolks and salt at medium speed until the mixture is light and fluffy, about 3 minutes.

3 In a small saucepan with a candy thermometer attached, combine the maple sugar with 1 tablespoon of water and bring to a boil. Cook over moderate heat, swirling the pan occasionally, until the syrup is very foamy and reaches 235°.

With the mixer at low speed, slowly drizzle the hot syrup down one side of the egg mixture and beat until the side of the bowl is cool to the touch, about 5 minutes.

4 Using a hand mixer, beat the chilled maple cream at medium speed until firm; fold into the egg mixture. Scrape the semifreddo into a 9-by-13-inch baking pan in an even layer. Freeze until firm, about 4 hours or overnight.

5 Serve the maple semifreddo in tall glasses layered with the candied pecans.

MAKE AHEAD

The semifreddo can be covered with plastic wrap and frozen for up to 1 week.

BUTTER-PECAN BLONDIE SUNDAES
WITH CREAMY CARAMEL SAUCE

SERVES **8**

TIME **Active 35 min; Total 1 hr 30 min**

BLONDIES

Nonstick baking spray

2 **cups all-purpose flour**

1 **tsp. baking powder**

¼ **tsp. baking soda**

½ **tsp. salt**

2 **sticks unsalted butter, softened**

1½ **cups light brown sugar**

½ **cup granulated sugar**

2 **large eggs**

1 **tsp. pure vanilla extract**

1 **cup pecan halves, chopped**

CARAMEL SAUCE

1¼ **cups sugar**

1 **cup heavy cream**

1 **Tbsp. unsalted butter**

Pinch of salt

SUNDAES

Butter-pecan ice cream and candied pecans, for serving

New York City pastry chef Bob Truitt loves anything that includes caramel and ice cream. "But there always needs to be a crunch," he insists. That's why he uses pecan-studded blondies as the base for this sundae and sprinkles candied pecans on top. Truitt makes his own candied nuts and ice cream, but store-bought work just as well.

1 MAKE THE BLONDIES Preheat the oven to 350° and coat a 9-by-13-inch baking pan with nonstick spray. In a small bowl, whisk the flour with the baking powder, baking soda and salt. In a stand mixer fitted with the paddle, beat the butter with the brown and granulated sugars at medium speed until fluffy. Add the eggs and vanilla and beat until smooth. Add the dry ingredients and beat at low speed until incorporated. Beat in the pecan halves. Spread the batter in the prepared pan and bake for about 30 minutes, until shiny and lightly crackled on top and the edges pull away from the sides of the pan. Let cool completely. Invert onto a board, cut into twelve 3-inch squares, then cut 8 of the squares into quarters (save the remaining squares for snacks).

2 MEANWHILE, MAKE THE CARAMEL SAUCE In a small saucepan, combine the sugar with ¼ cup of water and cook over moderate heat, stirring, until the sugar dissolves. Cook without stirring until a medium-amber caramel forms, about 5 minutes. Add the cream, butter and salt and simmer until thickened, about 2 minutes; let cool.

3 ASSEMBLE THE SUNDAES Divide half of the blondie pieces among 8 parfait glasses. Top with a scoop of ice cream and the remaining blondies. Sprinkle with candied pecans and drizzle with the caramel sauce. Garnish with more candied pecans and serve.

"I tasted this creamy, slightly sweet banana ice cream in our Test Kitchen one time and was instantly hooked. It's so easy to make and great in the summer, when I always seem to have an abundance of too-ripe bananas on hand." —SARA PARKS, PHOTO EDITOR

EASY BANANA ICE CREAM
WITH MILK CHOCOLATE CHUNKS

SERVES **4**

TIME **10 min plus 4 hr 30 min freezing**

3 ripe bananas

1¼ cups whole milk

⅓ cup sugar

1 tsp. pure vanilla extract

⅛ tsp. salt

½ cup heavy cream

3 oz. milk chocolate (preferably with nibs), chopped into ¼-inch chunks

For the simplest ice cream you'll ever make, NYC recipe developer Melissa Rubel Jacobson whips up the banana custard base in a blender, then pours it into an ice cream maker along with tasty chunks of milk chocolate.

1 In a blender, puree the bananas with the milk, sugar, vanilla and salt until smooth. Transfer to a large bowl and stir in the heavy cream and milk chocolate.

2 Pour the banana custard into an ice cream maker and freeze according to the manufacturer's instructions. Transfer the ice cream to an airtight container and freeze until firm, at least 4 hours. Let stand at room temperature for 10 minutes before serving.

FROZEN CHOCOLATE–CHIP MERINGATA

SERVES **8 to 10**

TIME **Active 1 hr;
Total 2 hr 30 min plus
10 hr cooling and freezing**

- 6 **large egg whites,
  at room temperature**
- ½ **tsp. cream of tartar**
- 1½ **cups granulated sugar**
- ½ **tsp. pure vanilla extract**
- 2¼ **cups heavy cream**
- ¼ **cup confectioners' sugar**
- 1 **lb. bittersweet chocolate,
  finely chopped**
- ¼ **cup hot brewed espresso**

Meringata is Italian for any type of dessert with meringue. Here, Rolando Beramendi, founder of Manicaretti Italian food importers, makes a homey yet elegant version by layering chocolate-chip cream between two large disks of meringue. After freezing the meringata, he slices it to serve with a warm chocolate-espresso sauce.

1 Preheat the oven to 225° and position racks in the lower and middle thirds. Trace an 11-inch circle on the underside of each of 2 sheets of parchment paper. Turn the paper over onto 2 large baking sheets.

2 In a stand mixer fitted with the whisk, beat the egg whites with the cream of tartar at medium speed until foamy. Increase the speed to high and beat until soft peaks form. Add the granulated sugar 1 tablespoon at a time, beating for 5 seconds between additions. Add the vanilla and beat until the whites are stiff and glossy, about 4 minutes.

3 Transfer half of the meringue to a pastry bag fitted with a ½-inch plain round tip and pipe a ring of meringue just inside each drawn circle. Spoon the remaining meringue into the circles and spread it ½ inch thick. Bake the meringues for about 1½ hours, until very pale but dry. Turn off the oven, prop the door open slightly and let the meringues cool in the oven for at least 6 hours, until dry and crisp.

4 In a medium bowl, using a hand mixer, beat 2 cups of the cream with the confectioners' sugar until firm. Fold in one-fourth of the chocolate. Spread the cream over 1 round, spreading it to the edge. Top with the second round, pressing it lightly. Freeze until the cream is firm, about 4 hours.

5 Melt the remaining chopped chocolate in a bowl set over a pan of simmering water. Off the heat, whisk in the remaining ¼ cup of cream and the espresso.

6 Using a serrated knife, cut the frozen cake into wedges and transfer to plates. Let stand for 10 minutes. Spoon some of the sauce on each wedge and serve.

CREAMY MOCHA ICE POPS

MAKES **10**

TIME **25 min plus 6 hr chilling and freezing**

2½ oz. dark chocolate, finely chopped

½ cup plus 1 Tbsp. sugar

½ cup ground medium-roast coffee (3 oz.)

1 cup heavy cream

Chopped toasted hazelnuts (optional)

📷 OPPOSITE PAGE

Actress Debi Mazar and her husband, chef Gabriele Corcos, hosts of the Cooking Channel's *Extra Virgin*, give these mocha ice pops a silky texture by folding whipped cream into the coffee-infused chocolate.

1 Line a sieve with cheesecloth. Put the chocolate in a heatproof bowl. In a medium saucepan, combine ½ cup of the sugar with the coffee and 1¾ cups of water and bring to a boil. Simmer over low heat for 4 minutes, stirring. Strain the coffee over the chocolate; whisk until melted. Let cool, then refrigerate the mocha mixture for at least 2 hours or overnight.

2 In a medium bowl, using a hand mixer, beat the cream with the remaining 1 tablespoon of sugar at medium speed until soft peaks form. Whisk the chilled mocha mixture until smooth, then fold in the whipped cream. Pour the mocha mixture into 10 ice pop molds and freeze for at least 4 hours. Press the frozen ice pops into the nuts, if using, and return them to the freezer for at least 30 minutes before serving.

ALMOST-INSTANT SOFT SERVE

MAKES **3½ cups**

TIME **15 min**

1½ lbs. frozen strawberries, mangoes or blueberries

¾ cup sweetened condensed milk

¼ tsp. vanilla extract

Kosher salt

We love this hack from F&W's Justin Chapple: Make ice cream with a soft-serve texture simply by pureeing frozen fruit with sweetened condensed milk in a food processor. Easy as that.

In a food processor, pulse the fruit with the sweetened condensed milk, vanilla and a generous pinch of salt until the fruit is finely chopped. Puree until smooth, 2 to 3 minutes; scrape down the bowl as needed.

Serve soft or transfer to a metal baking pan, cover and freeze until just firm.

MAKE AHEAD

The soft serve can be frozen for up to 3 days. Let stand at room temperature for 10 minutes before serving to your rabid crowd.

ROSEWATER-AND-SAFFRON ICE CREAM (BASTANI IRANI)

MAKES About 1 qt

TIME 45 min plus 8 hr chilling and freezing

6 large egg yolks

1½ cups heavy cream

1½ cups whole milk

¾ cup sugar

½ tsp. kosher salt

½ tsp. saffron, finely ground

¼ cup pure rosewater, preferably Sadaf brand (see Note)

½ tsp. pure vanilla extract

   Dried roses, for garnish

NOTE

Using a high-quality, pure rosewater is essential here. Look for Sadaf brand, which is available at kalustyans.com.

In Iran, this ice cream is commonly sold sandwiched between two wafers, but it's equally delicious on its own. Mahin Gilanpour Motamed, an accomplished home cook and mother of F&W editor in chief Nilou Motamed, decorates hers with fragrant dried Mohammadi roses from the Isfahan province of Iran.

1 Set a medium bowl in a large bowl of ice water. In another medium bowl, beat the egg yolks until pale, 1 to 2 minutes.

2 In a medium saucepan, whisk the cream with the milk, sugar, salt and saffron. Bring to a simmer over moderate heat, whisking, until the sugar is completely dissolved. Very gradually whisk half of the hot cream mixture into the beaten egg yolks in a thin stream, then whisk this mixture into the saucepan. Cook the custard over moderately low heat, stirring constantly with a wooden spoon, until it is thick enough to lightly coat the back of the spoon, about 12 minutes; don't let it boil.

3 Strain the custard through a fine-mesh sieve into the bowl set in the ice water. Let the custard cool completely, stirring occasionally. Stir in the rosewater and vanilla. Press a piece of plastic wrap directly onto the surface of the custard and refrigerate until well chilled, at least 4 hours.

4 Pour the custard base into an ice cream maker and freeze according to the manufacturer's instructions. Transfer the ice cream to a chilled 9-by-4-inch metal loaf pan, cover and freeze until firm, at least 4 hours.

5 Serve the ice cream in bowls, garnished with dried roses.

> "Doctoring store-bought ice cream or sorbet is my entertaining ace in the hole, too. This recipe gives lemon sorbet a special upgrade with layers of strawberry-vanilla puree and whipped cream."
> —JUSTIN CHAPPLE, TEST KITCHEN DEPUTY EDITOR

STRAWBERRY, LEMON AND VANILLA ICE CREAM PARFAITS

SERVES **4**

TIME **30 min**

- 1 lb. strawberries, hulled and quartered
- ¼ cup sugar
- 1 Tbsp. fresh orange juice
- ½ tsp. pure vanilla extract
- ¾ cup heavy cream
- 1 pint vanilla ice cream
- 4 graham crackers, coarsely crushed
- 1 pint lemon sorbet

New York City recipe developer Melissa Rubel Jacobson transforms store-bought ice cream into this impressive no-cook dessert. She layers refreshing lemon sorbet and vanilla ice cream with a simple fresh strawberry sauce, adding crushed graham crackers for a great crunch. Don't have parfait glasses? Spoon this no-fuss dessert into tall glasses or Mason jars.

1 In a food processor, combine the strawberries with the sugar, orange juice and vanilla and pulse until the strawberries are coarsely chopped. Let stand until the strawberries release some of their juice, about 10 minutes. Process the strawberries until smooth.

2 In a medium bowl, using a hand mixer, beat the cream at medium speed until soft peaks form.

3 Spoon 2 tablespoons of the strawberry sauce into each of 4 parfait glasses. Top with a scoop of vanilla ice cream, a sprinkling of the crushed graham crackers, a scoop of the lemon sorbet and another 2 tablespoons of the strawberry sauce. Top the parfaits with a dollop of the whipped cream and finish with a sprinkling of the graham crackers. Serve immediately.

AMERICAN-STYLE VANILLA BEAN ICE CREAM

MAKES 3½ cups

TIME Active 20 min; Total 1 hr 20 min plus 4 hr freezing

- 2 cups whole milk
- 1 Tbsp. plus 1 tsp. cornstarch
- 1½ oz. cream cheese, softened (3 Tbsp.)
- 1¼ cups heavy cream
- ⅔ cup sugar
- 1½ Tbsp. light corn syrup
- 1 vanilla bean, split and seeds scraped
- ⅛ tsp. kosher salt

Jeni Britton Bauer, founder of Jeni's Splendid Ice Creams, loves this exceptionally creamy American-style ice cream, which is much easier to make than the custardy French style. Instead of using egg yolks, her recipe relies on two unexpected ingredients: cornstarch (to help thicken it) and cream cheese (to soften it and make it scoopable).

1 Fill a large bowl with ice water. In a small bowl, mix 2 tablespoons of the milk with the cornstarch. In another large bowl, whisk the cream cheese until smooth.

2 In a large saucepan, combine the remaining milk with the heavy cream, sugar, corn syrup and vanilla bean and seeds. Bring to a boil and cook over moderate heat until the sugar dissolves and the vanilla flavors the milk, about 4 minutes. Off the heat, gradually whisk in the cornstarch mixture. Return to a boil and cook over moderately high heat until slightly thickened, about 1 minute.

3 Gradually whisk the hot milk mixture into the cream cheese until smooth. Whisk in the salt. Set the bowl in the ice water bath and let the ice cream base stand, stirring occasionally, until cold, about 20 minutes.

4 Strain the ice cream base into an ice cream maker and freeze according to the manufacturer's instructions. Pack the ice cream into a plastic container.

5 Press a sheet of plastic wrap directly onto the surface of the ice cream and close with an airtight lid. Freeze until firm, about 4 hours.

FRENCH-STYLE ICE CREAM

MAKES About 1 qt

TIME 25 min plus 4 hr 30 min
chilling and freezing

6 large egg yolks
¾ cup sugar
1¾ cups heavy cream
1¼ cups whole milk
Pinch of salt

This traditional ice cream with an egg-rich custard base is from Molly Moon and Christina Spittler, authors of *Molly Moon's Homemade Ice Cream.* The egg yolks help prevent ice crystals and make for a smooth, silky ice cream. For stir-ins or sundae toppings, Spittler says "nuts, butterscotch and caramel go great with that custardy flavor profile."

1 Set a medium bowl in a large bowl of ice water. In another medium bowl, whisk the egg yolks with ½ cup of the sugar until pale, about 3 minutes.

2 In a medium saucepan, combine the cream, milk, salt and remaining ¼ cup of sugar and bring to a simmer, whisking until the sugar is completely dissolved. Whisk the hot cream mixture into the beaten egg yolks in a thin stream.

3 Transfer the cream-and-egg mixture to the saucepan and cook over moderately low heat, stirring constantly with a wooden spoon, until the custard is thick enough to lightly coat the back of the spoon, about 4 minutes; don't let it boil. Pour the custard through a fine-mesh strainer into the bowl in the ice water. Let cool completely, stirring frequently. Refrigerate the custard until very cold, at least 1 hour.

4 Pour the custard into an ice cream maker with flavorings, if using, and freeze according to the manufacturer's instructions. Transfer the frozen custard to a plastic container, cover and freeze until firm, at least 3 hours.

"This is definitely 'big spoon ice cream,' the kind that's rich, custardy and lush and so worth making at home so you can have seconds. I love letting it sit out so it's a little soft and serving it with barely sweet, vanilla-roasted rhubarb and strawberries."
—JAMES MAIKOWSKI, ART DIRECTOR

"This is definitely not the ubiquitous low-fat fro-yo you find at self-serve joints. This delicious version has whole-milk yogurt, fresh lemon juice and a touch of cream. One little scoop is surprisingly rich and satisfies any sweet cravings."

—KATE HEDDINGS, EXECUTIVE FOOD EDITOR

LEMON-BLUEBERRY FROZEN YOGURT

MAKES **5 cups**

TIME **Active 30 min; Total 1 hr 30 min plus 4 hr freezing**

½ cup fresh lemon juice plus 1 Tbsp. finely grated lemon zest

One ¼-oz. package unflavored powdered gelatin

⅔ cup plus 6 Tbsp. sugar

¼ cup light corn syrup

2 cups plain whole-milk yogurt

½ cup heavy cream

¾ cup blueberries

"I never make frozen yogurt as a low-fat replacement for ice cream," says ice cream innovator Jeni Britton Bauer. Instead, she likes using yogurt to bring out the natural tanginess of fruits like lemons and strawberries.

1 Fill a large bowl with ice water. Pour 2 tablespoons of the lemon juice into a small bowl. Sprinkle the gelatin over the juice and let stand for 5 minutes.

2 Meanwhile, in a small saucepan, whisk the remaining 6 tablespoons of lemon juice with ⅔ cup of the sugar and the corn syrup. Bring to a boil and cook over moderate heat until the sugar dissolves, about 1 minute. Remove from the heat and stir in the lemon gelatin.

3 In a medium bowl, mix the yogurt with the lemon zest. Stir in the lemon juice mixture, then whisk in the cream. Set the yogurt base in the ice water bath and let stand, stirring occasionally, until cold, about 20 minutes.

4 Meanwhile, in a small saucepan, mix the blueberries with the remaining 6 tablespoons of sugar and 2 teaspoons of water. Simmer over moderate heat until saucy, about 4 minutes. Let cool.

5 Pour the lemon yogurt into an ice cream maker and freeze according to the manufacturer's instructions.

6 Scoop alternating spoonfuls of the yogurt and blueberry sauce into a plastic container. Press a sheet of plastic wrap directly onto the surface and close with an airtight lid. Freeze until firm, about 4 hours.

MATCHA MOCHI ICE CREAM SANDWICHES

MAKES **Twelve 2-inch ice cream sandwiches**

TIME **Active 45 min; Total 2 hr 30 min**

Cornstarch, for dusting

1½ cups sweet glutinous rice flour (mochiko flour)

1¼ cups water

¾ cup sugar

2 tsp. matcha powder

¼ tsp. kosher salt

1½ pints (3 cups) green tea ice cream, softened slightly

📷 PAGE 230

NOTE

For fun flavor variations like coconut and strawberry, go to foodandwine.com/mochi.

New York City pastry chef Jen Yee packs a double dose of antioxidants in these craveable ice cream sandwiches. She layers green tea ice cream between rounds of pastel-colored mochi—a simple Japanese dough that combines glutinous rice flour, sugar and the green-tea powder matcha.

1 Using a damp cloth, wipe down a large work surface. Lay a 14-inch sheet of plastic wrap on the surface and smooth it out with the damp cloth. Sift a generous layer of cornstarch on the plastic. Dust a large rimmed baking sheet with cornstarch.

2 In a large microwave-safe bowl, mix the rice flour, water, sugar, matcha powder and salt. Cover the bowl tightly with plastic wrap and microwave at high power for 2 minutes, until the batter starts to thicken around the edge. Remove the plastic and stir the mixture with a rubber spatula until it is mostly smooth; a few small lumps are OK. Re-cover the bowl and microwave at high power for 2 minutes; the dough should be stiff and sticky. Using the rubber spatula, stir the dough quickly and vigorously until smooth, about 30 seconds.

3 Working quickly, scrape the mochi dough out onto the prepared work surface and sift a fine layer of cornstarch over it. Pat the dough into a 9-inch round. Using a rolling pin lightly dusted with cornstarch, roll out the dough ¼ inch thick.

4 Dip a 2-inch round cutter in cornstarch and stamp out 24 rounds, rerolling the scraps as needed. Transfer the mochi to the prepared baking sheet. Cover with plastic wrap and freeze until firm, about 1 hour.

5 Meanwhile, scrape the softened ice cream into a gallon-size resealable freezer bag. Using a small spatula, spread the ice cream evenly so it's about ¾ inch thick in the bag, then squeeze out any excess air and seal. Freeze until firm, about 1 hour.

6 Line a 12-cup muffin tin with paper or foil liners. Using a pastry brush, dust the excess cornstarch off the mochi rounds. Place 1 mochi round in each cup. Lay the bag of ice cream flat on the counter and snip around the top of the bag, then peel it off. Using a 2-inch round cutter, stamp out 12 rounds of ice cream. Working quickly, lightly brush the 12 mochi in the muffin cups with water and top with the ice cream rounds. Brush each of the remaining 12 mochi rounds with water and set them damp side down on the ice cream. Press lightly to help the mochi and ice cream stick together. Freeze until firm, about 1 hour. Let the mochi sandwiches soften for about 10 minutes before serving.

MAKE AHEAD

The mochi ice cream sandwiches can be tightly wrapped individually in plastic and frozen for 1 week.

Matcha, Coconut and
Strawberry Mochi
Ice Cream Sandwiches,
p. 229

Ice Cream Birthday
Cake, p. 232

ICE CREAM BIRTHDAY CAKE

SERVES 16

TIME Active 1 hr 30 min;
Total 5 hr plus overnight
freezing

DEVIL'S FOOD CAKE

- **Nonstick cooking spray**
- 1 **cup all-purpose flour**
- ½ **tsp. baking powder**
- ½ **tsp. baking soda**
- ½ **tsp. kosher salt**
- ½ **cup plus 1 Tbsp. unsweetened cocoa powder**
- ½ **cup hot water**
- 4 **Tbsp. unsalted butter, at room temperature**
- 1¾ **cups dark brown sugar**
- 1 **large egg plus 1 large egg yolk**
- ½ **cup buttermilk**
- ½ **tsp. pure vanilla extract**

HOT FUDGE

- 1 **cup heavy cream**
- ¼ **cup plus 2 Tbsp. dark brown sugar**
- 4½ **Tbsp. unsweetened cocoa powder**
- ¼ **cup plus 2 Tbsp. light corn syrup**
- 9 **oz. bittersweet chocolate, coarsely chopped**
- 1½ **Tbsp. unsalted butter**
- ½ **tsp. kosher salt**

(continued on opposite page)

Laura Sawicki loves celebrating birthdays. At Launderette in Austin, she makes an epic layered ice cream birthday cake that's a nostalgic nod to the Carvel and Baskin-Robbins creations she adored as a kid. Her recipe—with a devil's food base, cold hot fudge, chocolate crunchies and a seriously thick chocolate ganache glaze— will make even the most die-hard chocoholics swoon.

1 MAKE THE DEVIL'S FOOD CAKE Preheat the oven to 350°. Spray an 8-inch springform pan with nonstick spray. In a medium bowl, whisk the flour with the baking powder, baking soda and salt. In a small bowl, whisk the cocoa powder with the water until a smooth paste forms. In the bowl of a stand mixer fitted with the paddle, beat the butter with the brown sugar at medium speed for 3 minutes. Beat in the egg, egg yolk, buttermilk and vanilla. At low speed, beat in the dry ingredients and cocoa paste in 2 alternating batches. Scrape the batter into the prepared pan and bake for 30 to 35 minutes, until a toothpick inserted in the center comes out with a few moist crumbs attached. Let the cake cool for 15 minutes, then remove the ring and let the cake cool completely on a rack. Leave the oven on.

2 Using a serrated knife, cut a ¼-inch-thick layer off the top of the cake. In a food processor, pulse the cake layer until fine crumbs form. Spread the crumbs on a small rimmed baking sheet and bake for 10 to 12 minutes, turning the pan halfway through, until the crumbs are crisp. Let the crunchies cool completely.

3 MAKE THE HOT FUDGE In a small saucepan, combine the cream with the brown sugar, cocoa powder and corn syrup and bring to a boil over moderate heat, whisking constantly. Reduce the heat to low and simmer for 1 minute. Remove from the heat and add the chocolate, butter and salt; whisk until smooth. Scrape the hot fudge into a bowl and let cool to room temperature.

4 ASSEMBLE THE CAKE Using scissors, trim a sheet of clear acetate to 6 by 24 inches. Wrap the acetate around the cake and secure it with tape. Secure the springform pan ring around the acetate-wrapped cake.

5 Using an offset spatula, spread half of the hot fudge evenly over the cake and top with half of the cake crunchies. Freeze until the fudge is firm, about 20 minutes. Using the spatula, spread the chocolate chip ice cream over the fudge layer and top with the remaining cake crunchies; press down to help them adhere. Freeze the cake for 20 minutes, until firm.

CAKE ASSEMBLY

2 **pints chocolate chip ice cream, softened slightly**

2 **pints strawberry ice cream, softened slightly**

2½ **cups heavy cream, chilled**

3 **Tbsp. granulated sugar**

8 **oz. bittersweet chocolate, coarsely chopped**

Maraschino cherries and rainbow sprinkles, for decorating (optional)

PAGE 231

6 Remove the cake from the freezer and spread the remaining hot fudge over the crunchies. Freeze for 20 minutes. Spread the strawberry ice cream over the fudge and freeze for another 20 minutes.

7 In a stand mixer fitted with the whisk, beat 1½ cups of the heavy cream with the granulated sugar until it holds soft peaks. Spread 2 cups of the whipped cream over the strawberry ice cream layer; refrigerate the rest of the whipped cream for decorating. Freeze the cake overnight.

8 Place the chocolate in a medium heatproof bowl. In a small saucepan, bring the remaining 1 cup of heavy cream to a boil. Pour the hot cream over the chocolate and let stand until melted, about 5 minutes. Stir until smooth, then tap the bowl on the counter to pop any air bubbles. Let the ganache cool down to 80°, about 30 minutes.

9 Carefully remove the springform ring and peel the acetate off the cake. Transfer the cake to a rack set over a rimmed baking sheet. Working quickly, pour the ganache onto the center of the cake in one fluid motion, allowing the excess to drip over the sides. Freeze the cake until the ganache is firm, about 30 minutes.

10 Meanwhile, whisk the reserved whipped cream until stiff peaks form. Transfer to a pastry bag fitted with a star tip. Pipe whipped cream around the edge of the cake and garnish with maraschino cherries and rainbow sprinkles, if desired. Freeze the cake for 30 minutes before serving.

PREP AHEAD

The cake can be assembled through Step 9; once the ganache is firm, wrap the cake in plastic and freeze for up to 1 week. Decorate the cake the day you plan to serve it. For neat slices, use a hot, sharp knife and wipe it off between cuts.

"This mega ice cream cake puts all others to shame! Since it serves 16 people, it's worth the effort—even if you don't intend to serve it to a crowd, it keeps in the freezer for days and days."

—KATE HEDDINGS, EXECUTIVE FOOD EDITOR

CARDAMOM-OATMEAL COOKIE ICE CREAM SANDWICHES

MAKES **10**

TIME **Active 30 min;**
Total 1 hr 30 min

¾ cup all-purpose flour
1 tsp. ground cardamom
1 tsp. kosher salt
½ tsp. baking soda
1 stick unsalted butter, softened
¾ cup packed light brown sugar
1 large egg
¼ cup buttermilk
1 tsp. pure vanilla extract
1½ cups old-fashioned
   rolled oats
1 pint ice cream, for filling

Cruze Farm in Knoxville, Tennessee, is famous for its outstanding ice creams, which the dairy sells from its food truck. These spiced-just-right oatmeal cookies are from Colleen Cruze Bhatti, who helps run the farm. They're the perfect texture for ice cream sandwiches—chewy and soft.

1 Preheat the oven to 350° and position racks in the lower and upper thirds. Line 2 large baking sheets with parchment paper.

2 In a medium bowl, whisk the flour, cardamom, salt and baking soda. In a large bowl, using a hand mixer, beat the butter with the sugar at medium-high speed until fluffy, 1 to 2 minutes. At medium speed, beat in the egg. Beat in the buttermilk and vanilla until just smooth, then beat in the dry ingredients. Fold in the oats.

3 Using a 2-tablespoon ice cream scoop, scoop 10 mounds of dough onto each baking sheet, about 2 inches apart. Bake for about 13 minutes, until the cookies are puffy and set; shift the sheets halfway through baking. Transfer the cookies to racks to cool completely.

4 For each ice cream sandwich, scoop 3 tablespoons of the ice cream onto the underside of a cookie and top with another cookie. Wrap in plastic and freeze until the ice cream is just firm, about 30 minutes.

LEMON AND FRESH SORREL SHERBET

MAKES	About 1 qt
TIME	30 min plus 5 hr chilling and freezing

1¼ tsp. unflavored powdered gelatin

1 cup fresh lemon juice

1½ cups sugar

2¼ cups whole milk

5 large sorrel leaves

2 tsp. finely grated lemon zest

After doing a foraging internship at the renowned Noma restaurant in Copenhagen, Belinda Leong of B. Patisserie in San Francisco started to incorporate wild greens and herbs into her desserts. When sorrel's in season, she uses the tart, lemony green to flavor her tangy sherbet, but mint, thyme and basil are terrific as well.

1 In a small bowl, sprinkle the gelatin over the lemon juice and let stand until softened, about 5 minutes.

2 In a medium saucepan, combine the sugar with 1½ cups of water and bring to a boil. Simmer over moderate heat until the sugar is dissolved, 2 to 3 minutes. Remove from the heat and whisk in the lemon juice mixture. Let cool completely, then refrigerate until chilled, about 2 hours.

3 In a blender, combine the lemon mixture with the milk and sorrel and puree until almost smooth, about 30 seconds. Strain the mixture through a fine sieve into a bowl and stir in the lemon zest.

4 Pour the sherbet mixture into an ice cream maker and freeze according to the manufacturer's instructions. Transfer to an airtight container, cover and freeze until firm, at least 2 hours, before serving.

VARIATION

For a bright lemon and mint sherbet, replace the sorrel with ½ cup of lightly packed mint.

Candies
& Sauces

CHOCOLATE CORN-FLAKE CLUSTERS

MAKES **About 4 dozen clusters**

TIME **40 min**

1 lb. semisweet or bittersweet chocolate, chopped into ½-inch pieces

4 cups corn flakes

NOTE

If your kitchen is very hot, you can refrigerate the finished clusters on the baking sheet for about 5 minutes to allow the chocolate to harden. Do not chill them for more than 10 minutes; if they get too cold, condensation will form on the surface when they are removed from the refrigerator, causing the chocolate to turn white. While this doesn't affect the taste, it does ruin the appearance.

Gifting homemade candies, such as these chocolate-covered corn flakes from master NYC chocolatier Jacques Torres, will make you super popular with your friends. For the best flavor and glossiest sheen, Torres advises tempering high-quality chocolate like Valrhona or Callebaut. Also, be sure to start with a fresh box of corn flakes for the crispest clusters.

1 In a microwave-safe bowl, heat two-thirds of the chocolate pieces for 30 seconds at high power, then stir with a rubber spatula. Continue to microwave the chocolate for 30 seconds at a time, stirring in between, until fully melted.

2 Stir in the remaining one-third of chocolate until melted. The melted chocolate should now register between 104° and 113° on an instant-read thermometer. If you don't have an instant-read thermometer, a simple method of checking tempering is to apply a small quantity of chocolate to a piece of paper or to the point of a knife. If the chocolate has been correctly tempered, it will harden evenly and show a good gloss within 5 minutes.

3 Pour the corn flakes into a large bowl, then pour about half of the tempered chocolate over them. Using a rubber spatula, quickly fold the corn flakes into the chocolate until they're evenly coated. The tempered chocolate will immediately begin to set. Once the chocolate has set, repeat with the remaining chocolate to give the corn flakes a second coat. Using a spoon, quickly scoop small mounds of the chocolate-covered corn flakes onto a parchment paper–lined baking sheet. Allow the chocolate to harden, then serve.

MAKE AHEAD

Store the corn-flake clusters in an airtight container in a cool, dry place. They will keep for 2 weeks (if you can resist eating them).

CHOCOLATE–ALMOND SALTINE TOFFEE

MAKES **2½ lbs**

TIME **40 min**

1½ cups sliced almonds (6 oz.)

Approximately 60 saltine crackers (not low-sodium)

1½ cups sugar

3 sticks unsalted butter

2 Tbsp. light corn syrup

½ lb. bittersweet chocolate, chopped into ½-inch pieces

Pastry chef Nicole Plue, director of pastry arts at San Francisco Cooking School, was intrigued by a recipe she discovered for matzo covered in toffee and chocolate. She improved the treat by using saltine crackers instead of matzo for a hit of salt. Now the buttery toffee is a consistent favorite on her petit four tray.

1 Preheat the oven to 350°. Spread the almonds on a baking sheet and toast for about 6 minutes, until golden.

2 Line a 12-by-17-inch rimmed baking sheet with a silicone mat or lightly buttered parchment paper. Arrange the saltine crackers on the baking sheet in a single layer, patching any holes with cracker bits; slight gaps are OK.

3 In a medium saucepan, combine the sugar, butter and corn syrup and cook over low heat until the sugar is melted. Brush the sides of the pan with a moistened pastry brush to wash down any sugar crystals. Cook the syrup over moderate heat without stirring until it starts to brown around the edge, about 5 minutes. Insert a candy thermometer into the syrup and simmer, stirring with a wooden spoon, until a honey-colored caramel forms and the temperature reaches 300°, about 6 minutes longer.

4 Slowly and carefully pour the caramel over the crackers, being sure to cover most of them evenly. Using an offset spatula, spread the caramel to cover any gaps. Let cool for 3 minutes, then sprinkle the chopped chocolate evenly on top. Let stand until the chocolate is melted, about 3 minutes, then spread the chocolate evenly over the toffee. Spread the almonds evenly over the chocolate. Freeze the toffee until set, about 15 minutes.

5 Invert the toffee onto a work surface and peel off the mat or paper. Invert again, break into large shards and serve.

MAKE AHEAD

The saltine toffee can be refrigerated for up to 2 weeks in an airtight container.

DARK CHOCOLATE BARK
WITH ROASTED ALMONDS AND SEEDS

MAKES **25 pieces**

TIME **30 min**

- 1 **lb. dark chocolate (60% to 70%), finely chopped**
- 1¼ **cups roasted whole almonds**
- ¾ **cup salted roasted pumpkin seeds and sunflower seeds**

"I'm more addicted to chocolate than I am to sugar," says master chocolatier Jacques Torres. A small piece of this super-chunky dark chocolate bark satisfies his intense cravings.

1 Line a baking sheet with parchment paper. In a bowl set over a saucepan of gently simmering water, heat the chocolate, stirring occasionally, until it is about two-thirds melted; do not let the bowl touch the water. Remove the bowl from the saucepan and stir the chocolate until it is completely melted and the temperature registers 90° on a candy thermometer. If the chocolate has not melted completely and is still too cool, set it over the saucepan for 1 or 2 minutes longer, stirring constantly; do not overheat.

2 Stir the almonds and seeds into the chocolate and spread onto the prepared baking sheet in a ½-inch-thick layer, making sure the nuts and seeds are completely covered in chocolate. Refrigerate the bark until hardened, 10 minutes. Invert the bark onto a work surface. Remove the parchment paper, break into 25 pieces and serve.

MAKE AHEAD

The broken bark can be stored in an airtight bag or container at cool room temperature for up to 10 days.

BEST-EVER NUT BRITTLE

MAKES **2 lbs**

TIME **20 min plus cooling**

- 2 cups sugar
- 1 stick unsalted butter
- ⅓ cup light corn syrup
- ½ tsp. baking soda
- 12 oz. roasted salted peanuts, cashews, pistachios and/or pecans

  Fleur de sel or crushed Maldon sea salt

Former F&W executive food editor Tina Ujlaki adapted this crunchy, buttery, slightly salty brittle from a recipe by pastry chef Karen DeMasco of New York City's Hearth. When her children were younger, Tina would make it as a holiday gift for their teachers. As she recalls, "Come November, I'd start getting these looks from teachers who were hoping for the brittle but too shy to ask for it."

In a large saucepan, combine the sugar, butter, corn syrup and ½ cup of water and bring to a boil. Cook over moderately high heat, stirring occasionally, until the caramel is light brown and registers 300° on a candy thermometer, about 10 minutes. Remove from the heat and carefully stir in the baking soda. The mixture will bubble. Stir in the nuts, then immediately scrape the brittle onto a large rimmed nonstick baking sheet. Using the back of a large spoon (oil it lightly if it sticks), spread the brittle into a thin, even layer. Sprinkle the brittle with salt and let it cool completely, about 30 minutes. Break the brittle into large shards and serve.

MAKE AHEAD

The brittle can be stored in an airtight container at room temperature for up to 1 month.

"My dentist is not impressed by my devotion to this recipe, but it's so addicting (especially when really good roasted Virginia peanuts are involved). I find that warming up the baking sheet slightly in a low oven makes the brittle easier to spread."
—JAMES MAIKOWSKI, ART DIRECTOR

CHOCOLATE-TAHINI FUDGE

MAKES	**About 80 pieces**
TIME	**45 min plus 2 hr chilling**

¾ **cup whole milk**

6 **Tbsp. unsalted butter**

3 **cups sugar**

12 **oz. dark chocolate (70%), finely chopped**

¼ **cup tahini**

2 **Tbsp. toasted sesame oil**

1 **Tbsp. hot water (optional)**

2 **cups Marshmallow Fluff (8 oz.)**

1½ **tsp. pure vanilla extract**

2 **Tbsp. lightly toasted sesame seeds**

Flaky sea salt

At the end of a meal, Boston pastry chef John daSilva loves to pass around tiny squares of this luscious fudge, enriched with the earthy flavor of sesame paste.

1 Line a 9-inch square baking pan with parchment paper. In a medium saucepan, combine the milk and butter and cook over moderate heat until the milk is hot and the butter is melted. Whisk in the sugar and cook, stirring occasionally, until the mixture reaches 240° on a candy thermometer, about 5 minutes.

2 Remove the saucepan from the heat. Add the chocolate, tahini and sesame oil and stir until the chocolate is completely melted. If the mixture separates, whisk in the hot water until it is smooth again. Add the Fluff and vanilla and stir vigorously until the Fluff is completely incorporated.

3 Scrape the fudge into the prepared pan and smooth the surface. Sprinkle with the toasted sesame seeds and let cool, then refrigerate until cold, about 2 hours. Cut into 1-inch squares, sprinkle with sea salt and serve.

"I never met a fudge I liked until this one. Tahini and a sprinkle of salt on top save it from getting cloying, which is the tragic downfall of most fudges. The creamy, nutty squares are best cold. I keep mine in the freezer so they don't get too melty."

—SUSAN CHOUNG, BOOKS EDITOR

MIRACLE PEANUT BUTTER CRUNCH

MAKES **About 3 dozen pieces**

TIME **20 min plus cooling**

- 1 **cup sugar**
- ¾ **cup light corn syrup**
- 1 **Tbsp. unsalted butter**
- 1½ **cups natural peanut butter**
- 1 **cup coarsely chopped roasted peanuts**
- ¾ **tsp. kosher salt**
- ¾ **tsp. pure vanilla extract**
- ½ **tsp. baking soda**

Mirracole Morsels in Kingston, Washington, makes peanut butter candies that are as flaky as the inside of a Butterfinger bar. The secret to the light, layered texture, says owner Nicole Haley, is the aerating power of baking soda. Incredibly, this super-giftable candy takes just 20 minutes to make, and the only special equipment you need is a candy thermometer. Be sure to buy the freshest, highest-quality peanut butter and peanuts that you can find.

1 Line a 9-inch square pan with foil. In a medium saucepan, stir the sugar with the corn syrup and 2 tablespoons of water. Add the butter and bring to a boil over high heat, stirring to dissolve the sugar. Attach a candy thermometer to the pan and cook over moderately high heat until the caramel reaches 285°, about 10 minutes.

2 Meanwhile, in a large, heatproof, microwave-safe bowl, combine the peanut butter with the peanuts and salt. Heat the mixture in the microwave at high power until melted and hot, about 1½ minutes. Stir well.

3 In a small bowl, whisk the vanilla with the baking soda. As soon as the caramel reaches 285°, carefully stir in the baking soda mixture; the caramel will foam and bubble up.

4 Immediately pour the caramel into the melted peanut butter mixture and, using a heatproof spatula, fold together as quickly as possible. You want the mixtures to be combined but not homogenized; the candy will come together very fast.

5 Immediately scrape the hot candy into the prepared pan and press into a flat, even layer. Let cool completely. Peel off the foil and cut the candy into squares.

MAKE AHEAD

Cut or uncut, the candy can be stored in an airtight container at room temperature for up to 2 weeks.

SOFT APPLE-CIDER CARAMELS

MAKES 150 caramels

TIME Active 1 hr 45 min;
Total 2 hr 45 min plus
overnight chilling

2 qts. apple cider

Nonstick cooking spray

3 cups heavy cream

½ cup sweetened condensed milk

4 cups sugar

¾ cup light corn syrup

1½ tsp. kosher salt

1 stick cold unsalted butter, diced

½ tsp. cinnamon

Pinch of ground allspice

Pinch of ground cloves

Neutral oil, such as canola or grapeseed, for brushing

F&W's Justin Chapple combines tangy-sweet cider with buttery caramel in these chewy treats. They're like bite-size candy apples. To add your own spin, use a flavored apple cider or different spices, like ground ginger or black pepper.

1 In a large saucepan, simmer the apple cider over moderate heat, stirring occasionally, until reduced to 1 cup, about 1 hour. Pour the reduced cider into a bowl.

2 Line a 9-by-13-inch baking pan with foil and coat the foil with nonstick spray. In a medium saucepan, combine the cream and sweetened condensed milk and bring to a simmer over moderate heat; keep the mixture warm over low heat.

3 In another large saucepan, combine the sugar with the reduced cider, corn syrup, salt and ¼ cup of water and bring to a boil. Simmer over moderate heat until the sugar dissolves, about 5 minutes. Carefully whisk in the butter until melted. Gradually whisk in the warm cream mixture until incorporated. Cook over moderately low heat, stirring frequently, until a golden caramel forms and the temperature

reaches 245° on a candy thermometer, about 45 minutes. Stir in the cinnamon, allspice and cloves and scrape the caramel into the prepared pan. Let cool completely, then refrigerate the caramel overnight.

4 Lightly brush a sheet of parchment paper with oil. Invert the caramel onto the parchment and peel off the foil. Using a sharp knife, cut the caramel into 1-inch-wide strips, then cut the block crosswise into ½-inch rectangles. Wrap each caramel in a square of parchment paper or a candy wrapper and twist the ends to seal. Serve or pack the caramels in boxes or tins.

MAKE AHEAD

The wrapped caramels can be stored in a cool spot or refrigerated for up to 2 weeks. The uncut caramel can be tightly wrapped in plastic and refrigerated for up to 2 weeks; cut just before serving.

ALMOND-PISTACHIO NOUGAT

MAKES About 2 lbs

TIME 1 hr plus cooling

- 3 cups roasted almonds
- ¾ cup unsalted shelled pistachios
  Nonstick cooking spray
- ¼ cup cornstarch
- ¼ cup confectioners' sugar
- 1⅔ cups plus 1 Tbsp. granulated sugar
- ¾ cup light honey
- 2 large egg whites, at room temperature
  Pinch of salt
  Neutral oil, such as canola or grapeseed, for greasing

NOTE

You will need two candy thermometers for this recipe.

Didier Murat makes this soft, chewy candy at Vergennes Laundry, his stellar café in western Vermont. (You can source it online under the Vadeboncoeur label.) The nougat is fantastic on its own or baked into croissants, a favorite of café co-owner and baker Julianne Jones. "The white part melts away, and it's like honey and nuts," she says.

1 Preheat the oven to 200°. Spread the almonds and pistachios on a large baking sheet and keep warm in the oven. Line an 8-inch square baking pan with parchment paper, allowing the paper to hang over on 2 opposite sides. Lightly coat the paper with nonstick spray. In a bowl, combine the cornstarch and confectioners' sugar and dust the pan with half of the mixture.

2 In a medium saucepan, combine the 1⅔ cups of granulated sugar with ¼ cup of the honey and 1¾ cups of water and boil until the sugar syrup registers 245° on a candy thermometer, 20 to 30 minutes. Continue cooking the sugar syrup until it reaches 305°, timing it so that you have it ready for the whipped egg whites and hot honey in the following steps.

3 Meanwhile, in a stand mixer fitted with the whisk, beat the egg whites with the salt until firm peaks form. Add the remaining 1 tablespoon of granulated sugar and beat until combined.

4 In a small saucepan, bring the remaining ½ cup of honey to a boil. When it reaches 265° on a candy thermometer, after 5 to 8 minutes, add it in a fast, steady stream to the egg whites with the mixer at medium-high speed. When the sugar syrup has reached 305°, add it to the egg whites in a fast, steady stream and beat at high speed until the mixture is pale, 3 to 5 minutes. Using an oiled wooden spoon, immediately stir in the hot nuts (the nougat will be a bit stiff).

5 Scrape the nougat into the prepared baking pan and, using oiled hands, press it into an even layer. Dust the remaining cornstarch mixture on top, cover with a sheet of parchment paper and let cool competely.

6 Lift the nougat from the pan and brush off the excess cornstarch powder. Using a serrated knife, cut the nougat into ¾-inch slices. Cut the slices in pieces and serve.

MAKE AHEAD

The nougat can be wrapped in wax paper and stored in an airtight container for up to 2 weeks.

LIGHT AND FLUFFY MARSHMALLOWS

MAKES **25 marshmallows**

TIME **40 min plus 3 hr setting**

1 Tbsp. plus 2 tsp. unflavored
   powdered gelatin
   Canola oil, for greasing
   Cornstarch, for dusting
1 cup sugar
2 Tbsp. light corn syrup
3 large egg whites

These incredibly airy, pillowy marshmallows from pastry whiz Dominique Ansel are made in the classic French style. Try them plain or with cinnamon, hazelnut or coconut-lime add-ins.

1 In a small bowl, mix the gelatin with ⅓ cup of water and let stand for 15 minutes. Meanwhile, grease an 8-inch square cake pan with oil and dust lightly with cornstarch, tapping out the excess.

2 In a small saucepan, mix the sugar with ⅓ cup of water and bring to a boil, stirring to dissolve the sugar. Add the corn syrup and cook over moderately high heat, without stirring, until the syrup registers 260° on a candy thermometer. Off the heat, stir in the gelatin mixture until dissolved.

3 In a stand mixer fitted with the whisk, beat the egg whites at medium-high speed until soft peaks form. With the machine on, drizzle the hot syrup into the egg whites in a very thin stream down the side of the bowl. Scrape the marshmallow into the prepared pan, smoothing the surface. Let stand until set, at least 3 hours.

4 Run a sharp knife around the marshmallow. Very lightly dust a work surface with cornstarch and invert the cake pan onto it, tapping to release the marshmallow. Using a lightly greased sharp knife, cut into 1½-inch pieces and serve.

VARIATIONS

Cinnamon Add ½ tsp. ground Vietnamese cinnamon during the last minute of beating the marshmallow; lightly dust the cut marshmallows with a sifted mixture of ⅔ cup cornstarch, ⅓ cup confectioners' sugar and 1 tsp. ground cinnamon.

Hazelnut Add ¼ cup hazelnut praline paste during the last minute of beating the marshmallow; coat the cut marshmallows in coarsely ground roasted hazelnuts.

Coconut-Lime Add 1 tsp. pure coconut extract and 2 tsp. finely grated lime zest during the last minute of beating the marshmallow; coat the cut marshmallows with toasted unsweetened shredded coconut.

BITTERSWEET TRUFFLES ROLLED IN SPICES

MAKES   **About 4 dozen truffles**

TIME   **Active 1 hr 30 min;
Total 2 hr 30 min**

- 1 **cup heavy cream**
- 3 **Tbsp. light corn syrup**
- ¾ **lb. bittersweet chocolate,
  finely chopped**
- 4 **Tbsp. unsalted butter, softened**
- ⅓ **cup finely shredded
  unsweetened coconut**
- ¼ **tsp. ground cardamom
  Pinch of ground cloves**
- ⅔ **cup plus 2 Tbsp. sugar**
- 1 **Tbsp. plus ¼ tsp. cinnamon**
- 1 **tsp. ground allspice**
- 1 **tsp. chipotle chile powder**
- 1 **tsp. ancho chile powder**
- ½ **cup unsweetened cocoa powder**
- ½ **tsp. five-spice powder**

**Joan Coukos of Manhattan's
Chocolat Moderne is a self-
taught chocolatier. She coats
her insanely rich truffles
with surprising ingredients,
including blends of Chinese
and Mexican spices.**

1 In a medium saucepan, bring the
cream and corn syrup to a boil.
Put the bittersweet chocolate in
a medium bowl and pour the
hot cream over it. Let stand for
2 to 3 minutes, then whisk
until smooth. Whisk in the butter.
Refrigerate the ganache until
firm, at least 1 hour.

2 Meanwhile, in a small dry skillet,
toast the coconut over moderate
heat, stirring constantly, until just
lightly browned, about 2 minutes.
Transfer to a small bowl and let
cool. Stir in the cardamom, cloves,
2 tablespoons of the sugar and
¼ teaspoon of the cinnamon. In
another small bowl, whisk ⅓ cup
of the sugar with the remaining
1 tablespoon of cinnamon, the
allspice and both chile powders. In
a third small bowl, whisk ¼ cup of
the cocoa with the five-spice
powder and the remaining ⅓ cup
of sugar. Put the remaining ¼ cup
of cocoa powder in another bowl.

3 Line a baking sheet with
parchment paper. Scoop up level
tablespoons of the ganache and
drop them onto the parchment.
Place the baking sheet in the
refrigerator for 10 minutes. Using
your hands, roll each mound of
ganache into a ball; you may have
to cool your hands in ice water
periodically while you work.

4 Roll 1 truffle at a time in 1 of the
coatings. Return the truffles to
the baking sheet, cover loosely
and refrigerate until chilled
before serving.

CARAMELIZED WHITE CHOCOLATE SPREAD

MAKES 1¼ cups

TIME 3 hr 20 min plus cooling

- ½ lb. Valrhona Ivoire, chopped (see Note)
- ½ cup heavy cream, warmed
  Salt

NOTE

White baking chocolate has just the right amount of cocoa butter for this recipe. It's available at specialty food shops and from amazon.com.

Slow-roasting makes the cocoa butter in white chocolate silky, rich and caramel-like. F&W's Justin Chapple was inspired by pastry chef Belinda Leong of San Francisco's B. Patisserie for this spread.

Preheat the oven to 225°. In a medium stainless steel bowl, bake the chocolate for 3 hours, stirring every 15 minutes, until golden. Gradually whisk in the warm cream and a generous pinch of salt. Let cool completely, then refrigerate until just spreadable, about 10 minutes.

SERVE WITH

Toasted rustic bread, sliced apples, sliced pears and strawberries.

MAKE AHEAD

The spread can be refrigerated for up to 5 days. Soften in the microwave for 10 seconds at a time, stirring in between, until just spreadable.

MISO CARAMEL SAUCE

MAKES **3 cups**

TIME **15 min**

1½ cups heavy cream

6 Tbsp. unsalted butter

1½ cups sugar

⅓ cup light corn syrup

½ cup shiro (white) miso

½ tsp. pure vanilla extract

At 42 Grams in Chicago, chef Jake Bickelhaupt makes an extraordinary 15-minute caramel sauce that's as versatile as it is delicious. Use it as a luxurious topping for vanilla ice cream or brioche French toast or blend it with soy milk for a milkshake.

1 In a small saucepan, combine the cream and butter and bring just to a simmer over moderate heat.

2 In a medium saucepan, mix the sugar, corn syrup and ¼ cup of water and cook over moderately high heat, without stirring, until the sugar is dissolved. Using a wet pastry brush, wash down any crystals from the sides of the pan. Continue to cook, gently swirling the pan occasionally, until an amber caramel forms, about 5 minutes.

3 Remove the pan from the heat and whisk in the cream mixture; it will bubble up. When the bubbles subside, very carefully pour the hot caramel into a heatproof blender. At medium speed, gradually blend in spoonfuls of the miso until incorporated. Transfer to a bowl and let cool, then whisk in the vanilla.

MAKE AHEAD

The caramel can be refrigerated for up to 1 week. Rewarm gently before serving.

"I was lucky enough to try this sauce on vanilla ice cream while our Test Kitchen was working on this recipe for our Best New Chefs story in 2015. I love the surprise hit of umami in the slightly salty caramel." —SARA PARKS, PHOTO EDITOR

CHOCOLATE SHELL

MAKES 2 cups

TIME 15 min

1 lb. bittersweet chocolate, finely chopped

½ cup coconut oil

Salt

📷 OPPOSITE PAGE

F&W's Justin Chapple upgrades the childhood favorite Magic Shell (the sauce that quickly hardens when poured over cold ice cream). Coconut oil adds a ton of extra flavor.

In a large microwave-safe bowl, heat the chopped chocolate with the coconut oil at high power for 20 seconds at a time, stirring in between, until melted. Stir in a generous pinch of salt and let stand at room temperature until cooled before using.

MAKE AHEAD

The chocolate shell can be stored in an airtight container at room temperature for 2 weeks.

ENDLESS CARAMEL CORN

MAKES 20 cups

TIME 30 min plus cooling

3 Tbsp. vegetable oil, plus more for greasing

½ cup popping corn

1½ tsp. baking soda

1 tsp. adobo sauce (from a can of chipotle chiles in adobo)

3 cups sugar

3 Tbsp. unsalted butter

1 Tbsp. kosher salt

Phoenix chef Stephen Jones created this salty, sweet and amazingly crisp caramel-coated popcorn. Its stealth hit of spice comes from the adobo sauce in canned chipotles.

1 Lightly coat a large bowl and 2 large rimmed baking sheets with oil. In a large saucepan, combine the 3 tablespoons of oil and the popping corn. Cover and cook over moderate heat until the corn starts to pop. Shake the pan and cook until the corn stops popping, about 5 minutes. Transfer the popcorn to the prepared bowl.

2 In a small bowl, whisk the baking soda with the adobo sauce. In a large saucepan, combine the sugar with the butter, salt and ½ cup of water and bring to a boil, stirring until the sugar dissolves. Boil over moderate heat without stirring until a golden caramel forms, about 13 minutes. Remove from the heat and stir in the adobo mixture; the syrup will foam. Immediately drizzle the hot caramel over the popcorn and, using 2 greased spoons, toss to coat. Spread the caramel corn on the prepared baking sheets and let cool completely before serving.

MAKE AHEAD

The caramel corn can be stored in an airtight container for up to 5 days.

RECIPE INDEX

Page numbers in **bold** indicate photographs.

PHOTO CREDITS